GHOST STORIES
AND LEGENDS OF
SOUTHWESTERN CONNECTICUT

GHOST STORIES
AND LEGENDS OF
SOUTHWESTERN CONNECTICUT

DONNA KENT

HAUNTED
AMERICA

Published by Haunted America
A division of The History Press
Charleston, SC 29403
www.historypress.net

First published 2009

Manufactured in the United States

ISBN 978.1.59629.689.3

Library of Congress Cataloging-in-Publication Data

Kent, Donna.
Ghost stories and legends of southwestern Connecticut / Donna Kent.
p. cm.
Includes bibliographical references (p.   ).
ISBN 978-1-59629-689-3
1. Ghosts--Connecticut. 2. Haunted places--connecticut. I. Title.
BF1472.U6K465 2009
133.109746--dc22
2009035773

This book is dedicated to Mr. Peet.

CONTENTS

ACKNOWLEDGEMENTS

As usual, where to begin? I have been overly fortunate to have been helped by so many people throughout and over the past thirteen years when the journey of this book first began. Special thanks to Michele Polvay, my "other sista," whose constant source of belief, support and sheer survival tactics have literally kept me going and whose selfless generosity makes her the closest thing to a saint that I'll probably ever meet, and I am very proud and lucky to have her as a friend.

Thank you to my family: Mom and Dad, who never failed to remind me that this "ghost kick" should not deter me from maintaining a "real job." They were, of course, correct, as much as I struggled against the facts. Thanks to my extended family—my "country cousins" Brian and Jerry, Aunt Muriel and Uncle Johnny—for all their help and research with me on the Peet family and especially all the laughs and spooky stories 'round the campfire on those chilly Pennsylvania nights since I was a little kid. Thanks to all the perfect children in my life: Chloe and Justin, again for bearing with me, to Jenna for her support and companionship as a Cosmic Society member and to Sheri for coming with me on a few late-night excursions to the bone yards and haunted places near the lake despite being totally creeped out by it all!

Loads of gratitude to all of my Cosmic Society members—past, present and future—for all of the time, money, endless support, understanding and all that they have contributed to make our society one of the leaders in our field, especially Margaret ("Margarick") Sholz, our Gettysburg expert and best damn chocolate fudge maker in the East, and Gregory Polletta, our Reiki master and all-around great guy. Thanks to Heather and Joe Cappozello for always driving and figuring out the technical difficulties. Thank you to Sherry Vail for making the trek from New York City every month for meetings regardless of the time, expense and travel. Thanks to Charlene and Brendan Logan for hangin' in there and always volunteering to help. Thanks to all of the members who helped write, edit and contribute their experiences and findings on the individual cases—always appreciated!

Benevolence and all the best to Joyce St. Germaine for being a constant source of inspiration and guidance; that woman is a true "light worker" and someone to be revered and respected.

A thank-you to Betty Cordellos of Haunted Connecticut Tours for always pushing me to commit to a date for scouting out locations—or else it just doesn't get done! Betty is the one other person I know whose workload-juggling skills rival my own, and she is to be commended.

Thank you to my extended family of friends whose thoughts, constructive criticism and honest outlook have kept me in check, and a special thank-you to Cherie Ferguson for help with formatting and editing this book (mistakes are all hers!) and drumming up readings for me when penniless. Thanks to cohort Laurie Lemay for making me think I was "working poolside" when, in fact, I was just enjoying relaxing for a day—need more of those!

Very, very special thanks to Freddy Graham ("Count Fredula") for giving me the physical space I needed to write the book, in the nick of time, for helping us move (again!) and for always coming to the rescue. You're the best. No, really! Thank you to everyone at The History Press for your guidance, patience and understanding and for really helping to make this book as I've envisioned it for the past fifteen years. I appreciate all that you have done and look forward to continuing the series in the near future; I will need some time to come up for air, first though!

I'd also like to thank all of the CosmicSociety.com web viewers who have, over the past fifteen years, sent in their stories, video/audio recordings and incredible spirit energy photographs.

To all the docents and staff of haunted restaurants and locations we visit, I would like also to express how grateful I am for the time spent telling your stories and experiences to me and for your open house policy extended to Cosmic Society and the trust you've placed in us by sharing not only your dwellings or properties but also the tales and lore of those places and of the people who figured prominently there in the past—specifically Bessie Burton, Paul and Debbie Sciarrafa, T.J. Hardisty and Judith Kelz. Appreciation is given to the tolerant neighbors of the locations and, above all, to the spirits that endlessly roam those places for reasons all their own.

THE NICHOLS FARMS BURIAL GROUNDS, INCLUDING MR. PEET

I've been asked "What's a nice girl like you doing in a cemetery like this?" Despite a lifelong fascination with all things strange, bizarre and otherworldly, my ordinary life seemed to change on Thursday, March 19, 1995; my family and I were returning home from a family birthday party in Trumbull, Connecticut. Driving along normally until just after we passed an old cemetery on the left side of the street, I suddenly had an overwhelming urge to get out of the car. *Something* was really insistent that I take photos in the tiny cemetery we happened to be passing. I had heard of spirit photography in the past but wanted to take some time doing research on the subject before actually doing it. The spirit that would appear in my photo dictated otherwise, as I would learn in the future. There were only two frames left on the roll of film in my camera that also contained shots from the birthday party. I got out and took a wide shot to include the sign and then zoomed in on a smaller area near the center-left of the graveyard. I completely forgot about them until they returned via mail from the developer.

I didn't really expect anything to come of it. Little did I know the photographic results were about to change my entire life in a multitude of ways! The images of a full-figured man, an angel and a pitchfork (none of which I had seen when taking the photo) appeared on the very last frame of film shot sometime between 5:00 and 6:00 p.m.

I began by researching in the town of Stratford because, early on, Trumbull was once part of the larger territory. On May 14, 1662, Joseph Judson received Trumbull as a gift from the Pequonnock Indians. In 1690, Abraham

This photo, taken on March 19, 1995, shows the image of a full-figured man, in spirit form, standing behind a tombstone with the last name of "PEET" on it. Also captured in the photo are an angelic figure and a two-tined pitchfork. This photo has been voted one of the top ten ghost photos of all time.

Nichols had the first permanent settlement, and six years later, what we now know as Nichols Avenue was built and named the Farm Highway. Trumbull was incorporated as a town in October 1797 and named for Revolutionary War governor Jonathon Trumbull, who was a friend and advisor to General George Washington. Trumbull was the only colonial governor to serve in office continually before and after the American Revolution.

The Trumbull Historical Society was helpful in providing an old parchment cemetery plot grid, written with feather quills, that helped me to locate the names etched on the tombstone in my photo. There were three: Abijah Peet, age fifty-four, died in 1805; Bethiah Peet, his wife, age seventy-seven, died in 1826; and son Philo, age forty-seven, died in 1826. Using the last name of "Peet" as my starting point on just who this "ghost man" (or, as I now refer to him, "Mr. Peet") could be, I headed to the Stratford Public Library. Luck would have it that in its reference section, it had a volume of Peet family ancestry more than eight hundred pages long. It was at this point when I stuck my finger into the book and flipped to a random page. Well, how strange that on that particular page was a word that jumped out and grabbed my eye. The word was "Coudersport." Coudersport happens to be a very small town in northwestern Pennsylvania. It also happens to be the very same small town from which my mother and her relatives hail and to which I have traveled almost every year of my childhood to spend weeks or months with my cousins and that side of the family. It was at this time I began to "feel" that there might be a connection between my family and the Peet family, although this was just a hunch. Had I not found that page randomly, it's doubtful that I would have ever figured out the unusual connection of the man in the gravestone to my relatives and to me.

However, one "coincidence" after another concerning my research fed my curiosity to continue each and every time I had resolved to give up; to find pertinent information on people who lived and died hundreds of years ago is *not* so easy unless they were extremely prominent people! No longer believing in coincidence, I began to record these synchronistic events. Although some of these occurrences may seem trivial or unimportant as you read them, they do actually fit into the scheme of things, as I was to later discover. I started a timeline.

Before the photo was even taken, I had attended my grandmother's funeral in Eulaliah Cemetery, Coudersport, Pennsylvania. It was February 1995, and I rented a car for the journey.

The photo was taken on March 19, 1995, at dusk.

In April 1995, I returned to Nichols Farms Burial Ground and located the stone behind which the ghost man had appeared using the original photograph as a guide. I took more photos of the gravestone and had them developed. Upon examination of these, and by turning one of the pictures sideways, I discovered the ghost man's face—the same face!—complete with mustache and hairline. It seemed to be formed in the moldy gook called lichen that had accumulated on the bottom of the tombstone. This was definitely not noticeable when I shot the picture. Also apparent in the photo are what look like bony fingers just under his chin and, lower still, an image of a wolf's head.

During the same month, I spent a weekend in Coudersport, Pennsylvania, for a cousin's wedding. Arriving late and without a gift, the only store open was a grocery store. As I pulled into the lot, I spotted the street sign. It was Peet Street.

The photograph would become a topic of conversation at the wedding reception, and I was informed of a "John Peet" who worked at the same hospital where my granny had died just a few months earlier. I decided to call him and had no idea how receptive he would be to the idea of a stranger showing up with a photo of one of his long-dead relatives; either he'd think I

This is the actual family tombstone that "Mr. Peet" was photographed standing behind. What's interesting here is that if viewed sideways (tilting bottom left corner up), the bottom of the gravestone shows a face (the same face of the full-figured ghost). Clearly a head with hair, eyes and mustache can be seen in the upper portion of the headstone. Less discernible are what look like bony fingers (under the chin) and, further below, a wolf's head.

was some kind of nut and would hang up in my face, or like most people he might have a ghost story or two of his own. His number was located less than an inch away from my relatives' number in a local phone directory. I held my breath after introducing myself and mentioning the photograph and a possible family connection. Luckily, he was open to the possibility of a spirit world and had experienced encounters within his home. It just so happened that this John Peet is an avid family historian (what are the chances?) who supplied me with his copy of his family tree, *and* he is also a caretaker of a small cemetery along with his hospital job, which was where he tended to my dying grandmother—we were meant to talk!

He met with me that evening after asking where I was staying. I told him the name of the hotel, and he informed me that "The Westgate" hotel sits on land previously owned by the Peets and that the Eulaliah Cemetery (directly across the street from the hotel), where my grandmother is buried, was land donated to the town by the Peet family for cemetery usage. I showed him my "Mr. Peet" photo, and he in turn displayed a picture of his brother who bears a strong resemblance to the ghostly image. He and I then drove over to Eulaliah Cemetery so I might take a few pictures, and he led me to his great-great-great-grandparents' gravesites. I got the coldest chill when I realized that I was looking at the gravestones of the people whose names I had turned to when first opening the Peet family book at the Stratford Library.

Research done in May 1995 at the Trumbull Historical Society revealed that Abijah Peet's body was moved from Unity Burial Ground (which is less than a mile down the road) to Nichols Farms Burial Ground shortly after 1806. Then I uncovered a discrepancy with Philo Peet's burial spot; records indicate that he is interred at Long Hill Cemetery in Trumbull, Connecticut, yet his name appears on the stone at Nichols Farms Burial Ground. Where is he really? I wondered if either of these peculiar situations could be the reason for the unrest. I still didn't know what this ghost man wanted from me. My notes from 1995 include this paragraph:

> *Since the first photograph (possibly even before) one event has led to another concerning this situation (chance meetings, coincidences, etc.). I feel as if something is leading me to and through these happenings for some particular reasons presently known only to them. At this time I still don't know what it is I'm supposed to find out or why—one possibility still unexplored is that my early ancestors (from PA) may have had something to do with the Peet family (who came from Stratford, CT [where I lived at the time] and traveled to Coudersport, PA). Maybe I'm linked with them somehow?*

Anyway there is some sort of unrest that needs to be brought to closure and my research is ongoing at present.

Then Mr. Peet appeared in my house one night in June 1995. While reaching into the refrigerator, I saw a bright light to the right of me. Turning to look, I saw standing against the wall the man from the photo. I could still see my telephone on the wall through the apparition. It was "Mr. Peet"; his arms were folded on his chest and he stared straight ahead. I froze and he disappeared.

In October 1996, I founded the Cosmic Society of Paranormal Investigation. People began writing and asking how they could become involved with the society as members. Then came the CosmicSociety.com website and the newsletter, *Cosmic Connections*, which I self-published quarterly for twelve years. Nowadays, I write books.

It was December 1996 when I was asked to film a segment with the SyFy channel's hit TV show *Sightings*, which had heard of the photo and wanted to combine spirit photography with documentation I had gotten on film during an investigation I was conducting in a private home.

I was introduced to a highly respectable psychic (now associate and friend), Joyce St. Germaine. She was immediately drawn to the photo of Mr. Peet and suggested we try sometime in the near future to contact him through channeling to find his reason for appearing in the picture. I agreed, eager to glean any information to be had, but still held my reservations about channeling in general.

A few months later, Joyce invited me to investigate the apartment of a troubled young woman to see if we could document any activity on film. She suggested I arrive a few hours early, and we would try to contact Mr. Peet. The information—gleaned through a subject who was hypnotized by Joyce and who willingly allowed his voice box to be utilized by Mr. Peet—was incredibly accurate and most definitely privy information. Only someone very adept in the knowledge of the situation could have conceivably known about this information.

The following is a transcript of a channeling session conducted by Joyce St. Germaine to air on her TV show *The Sacred Journey*.

I'd like to point out that some of the verbiage is consistent with that of the eighteenth century, and it was at times a bit difficult to decipher and understand. Some of it was unintelligible no matter how many times I rewound and relistened to the audio/videotape. I've left the speech intact and without correction as that was how it came through, and it's not up to me to change it. There were pauses between almost every single word spoken by the spirits being channeled, indicating that this process is one that takes some getting used to for the entities utilizing it. In some cases, there were very long pauses, and I've indicated these throughout the transcript. It was also difficult hearing Joyce at many points because she has such a soft, gentle tone of voice, consistent with that of a hypnotherapist.

In part one of the shows, Joyce and I discuss the photo of Mr. Peet, the other being perceived and the strange object in the photo. Joyce vouches for the dozens of photos of mine that she has seen and spirit photography in general. Addressing the camera, she begins by placing Paul Hoffman under hypnosis in an attempt to talk to Mr. Peet, the man from my photo. She says, "The reason I chose this particular photograph to explain more deeply is I really got a very strong feeling of a powerful connection between Donna and this gentleman. Whether it's present life or past life, I don't know yet, but we're going to talk with him to see if there's anything we can do for him or with him." Joyce's replies will follow a "J," Paul's will follow a "P," Mr. Peet's will follow "Mr. P," his father's will follow an "F" and Donna's will follow a "D":

> **J**: *Paul and I are ready to work, and he is in what would be considered a trance state of hypnosis. We are going to ask this spirit man to speak through him. Now, we are trying to document this in a lot of different ways, so you may hear cameras rewinding, see flashes of light in the background because Donna is trying to see if his energy form will appear in a still photograph that she takes. I want to stress that I always ask my subjects for their higher self or spirit self permission to do this kind of work. Paul, please ask your higher self for permission to do this type of work.*
>
> **P**: *All right.*
>
> **J**: *Paul, what I'd like you to do is focus on the photograph (mentally) we've been discussing and looking at. Try to tune into that era and location.*

[It is at this point that the tape recorder shuts off with a loud thud, and Joyce explains to TV audience about all the noises coming from the background. She explains that we have set up a gauss meter, compass, audio recorder, video camera, etc., to try to register any changes in electromagnetic fields and to try to capture any sort of activity on film. She states that whenever she does this kind of work, no one knows how long it will take or how quickly things will happen but that we are trying to do it within the constraints of a half-hour television program.]

J: *We are going to ask St. Michael the Archangel to stand by and protect the area and anyone involved with this case with a protective net of white light. And I'm going to ask that if it's for the highest good, I call upon and welcome this man to speak through Paul without harming anyone in any way, we'd very much like to talk to you.*

P: *I see him. He's been a traveler back and forth from the light.*

J: *So, he's not earthbound?*

P: *No.*

J: *Will he be willing to speak through you using your vocal cords?*

P: *Yes.*

J: *You'll find it easy to speak.*

Mr. P: *I was never here before, speaking this way.*

J: *In this way, meaning out loud and using the voice of someone else?*

Mr. P: *As I am now, using the voice of another.*

J: *Did you talk with people, communicate, um…what I'm talking about, as in their inner ears, so that they heard in more a spirit level, than a physical?*

Mr. P: *I have spoken and seen and shown who I have been. I have come for these many years to bring comfort to my father, who's been troubled all these years. And I have another reason that I am now showing; to come here and speak.*

J: *What is that reason?*

Mr. P: [Unintelligible] *While the woman was recording my visit, I was given word to seek her help, and* [unintelligible] *bring her to this place, to bring comfort and passing, to my father.*

J: *We will be able to help your father with that.*

Mr. P: *Yes, I know.*

J: *Did you know that Donna would be coming to where we are right now? And that we would be talking to you this way?*

Mr. P: *I saw this all at the time of our meeting.*

J: *It's interesting because when Donna and I met, we felt that it was just the beginning of a connection and something very powerful happened when I saw the photograph of you. As far as a connection, I'm glad we all listened to our inner voices. Would you like me to now talk with your father and help him find his way into the spirit planes, into the light? Or would you want to share more information with us?*

Mr. P: *If it's pleasing, you may speak with my father, as his life and death were mired in confusion and abrupt.*

J: *Is your name Mr. Peet? Are you one of the Peets in which is a father and son, Abijah and Philo?*

Mr. P: *Our names were shortened. We are from Europe, both my brother and I. My mother comes from Greece, my father from Italy.* [Long pause.] *We came here; my father could speak none of this language. And at a young age of seven and eight, my brother and I, father and mother, had chartered a ship, came to the shores of this place on the mouth of the river. And we began a small farm, and with the wealth that we did not lose all of, we began the growth of horses and tobacco.*

J: *Before we talk to your father and help him into the light, would you like to talk to Donna Kent?* [We switch places and I am almost beside myself with anticipation…In hindsight, I have now thought of all the questions I should have asked him, but at the time, was too excited!]

Mr. P: *I would.*

D: *Mr. Peet, I'd like to know: is your first name Philo?*

Mr. P: *My brother's first name is that.*

D: *What is your name?*

Mr. P: *Upon moving to this place my name was* [sounds like…Isaiah? Azira? Ira? Hiram?]

D: *And your father's name?*

Mr. P: *Upon moving to this place my father had changed his name to* [Ruk? Rook?]

D: *Ok, um, is there some connection between my relatives in Pennsylvania and yours?*

Mr. P: *Yes.*

D: *Can you tell me more on that? Extrapolate a bit on that? Did you see me when I went to my grandmother's funeral?*

Mr. P: *I was there. Our relation is through a sister, who was born after we arrived on these shores. She in time moved toward the west of this state, this territory, and again moved further west and raised a family. She married a farmer* [long pause] *and it is through this, that we are known to each other.*

D: *Are we related in some way?*

Mr. P: *Distantly.*

D: *Um, are you aware of the times when I come to the cemetery to try to photograph?*

Mr. P: *I am.*

D: *Did you make yourself purposely known to me in the photograph?*

Mr. P: *I did.*

D: *What can you tell me about the angel that I perceive in the photograph? Are you aware of that?*

Mr. P: *As a guide, I have been blessed with the assistance of this light being who is here to watch over me when I come from the bright light to visit the site of my troubled father.*

D: *Can you tell me why he's troubled? I think I might have an idea.*

Mr. P: *It was through one incident when he was younger. He was involved in a crime that has never left his conscious thoughts.*

D: *Did he harm someone?*

Mr. P: *He brought the end of someone's life in rage.*

J: *This is where we are going to be able to help.*

Here the show ends and we continue to film part two of the episode. Joyce opens with preliminaries:

J: *We continue with last week's show about Spirit Photography, or Psychic Photography. You remember we talked about some of the pictures that Donna Kent took in which a full-figured man made his presence known through the film.*

Joyce then goes on to talk about helping his father see that everyone who is involved in a situation chose that event for their spiritual growth and progress. She says "and you know at the beginning of this show, this gentleman said that he made himself visible in the photograph to you, knowing that eventually you and I would hook up and I would be able to hook up with his father, and we get lots of situations like that." And the show continues:

J: *So what we're going to do now is talk with his father like to be sure because that is the goal here to help his father out. I get the feeling it would be easier and easier for you to travel back and forth and talk with Donna; if it's for the highest good, would you be willing to come back again?*

Mr. P: *For a time, as my father passes on. Donna and I will meet less frequently. It is through her, and through her efforts, I am finished my work here, to continue on.*

J: *That was a nice compliment, Donna.*

D: *Yes.*

Mr. P: *My father was a hard and disciplined man. Although he never brought abuse, he rarely spoke to us. Yet my brother and I can grow strong and proud.*

D: *Can I ask you if you frequent some of the other places I have found concerning the Peet family or have gone to try and take photographs? At a certain house I found, used to belong to your family, that stands there now and also the Shakespeare Theater that stands there now, your property used to border that. Do you go there ever? Is that you sometimes in the photographs?*

Mr. P: *The essence of who I appeared was to make connection with you so that your work will continue and become greater and then in turn flower...become to a conclusion here.*

J: *Ok, we're going to continue on in a second show. I know that time is very different in the spirit planes, but here we have to work in a linear fashion. Please understand it was very important to establish the connection of why this gentleman came into Donna's life and what it really means. And now I think it's equally important we talk to his father and help his father into the light. We're going to continue filming, however; this portion will air on next week's show. I hope you'll continue to tune in as helping someone pass into the light is one of the greatest gifts I've ever been, I guess, blessed or privileged to use or to do.* [Joyce closes the show.]

While the camera was being readied for the second show, I questioned Joyce about the burial discrepancies I'd found through my research concerning Abijah and Philo Peet. I wondered out loud if this could have anything to do with the unrest going on, and Joyce squelched any notion of that by replying, "Where the physical body lies is so insignificant. His father has not gone on because of guilt, prevalent in our society, unfortunately, that keeps people from moving on."

Out there in "TV Land," it would appear as if a week had passed when they would be able to watch part two of the show, which we just continued to shoot. The second episode was opened and continued:

J: *Good Evening and welcome to* The Sacred Journey. *The Sacred Journey is a program that reminds us that life is a wonderful adventure and every experience is a perfect opportunity to learn.*

After recapping the previous show, Joyce asks Paul to get permission, once again from his higher self, and does all the prior protection procedures that should be followed before any attempts at spirit communication, including requesting protection again from St. Michael.

J: *I now call upon the father of this gentleman that we are talking to who needs our help getting to the light and allow him to speak through Paul, without harming him in any way.*

P: [Long pause and unintelligible mumbles.]

J: *Is this Paul talking? Or is this the father of the gentleman—that beautiful light being that we were just talking to? I call upon you and ask you to speak through Paul because I would like to offer my assistance to you. I'd like to help you find a place of peace, light and love.*

F: [Sounds like] *Maroque Petros.*

J: *Is that your name?*

F: *I came with my family and I have not forgotten.*

J: *Is there something that happened that is very painful for you and the memories of it can still continue to bring pain?*

F: *I have sanctioned the journey that we had taken. I came here away from the suspicions of the family that I harmed, but I cannot forget that it was my rage that wasted the life of my friend. That drunken rage.*

J: *Something has happened between that time and now that you probably haven't noticed. Many, many years, hundreds of years—*

F: [Unintelligible, sounds like] *No, no don't.*

J: *Something wonderful has happened* [that] *I would like to share with you. Many years have gone by, perhaps even hundreds of years, and your friend is very much alive. He's alive in the most important way. He's alive in spirit as you are, as your son is. I call upon the beautiful spirit essence of this friend of this man. Make his presence known and appear to him. Look for your friend. Do you see him?*

F: *I see him in many forms. I see him in many ways. I see that he has moved on. He had favor with thine* [unintelligible] *thine own crime, was a genuine crime.*

J: *This is what I was telling you, that the physical body is the most unimportant part of a person and that your friend chose to have that experience because perhaps at another time he had brought harm to someone and this was the best way to learn about it, to understand it and to bring balance.*

F: *I may understand this, but I learned that in avoiding the sentence which I deserved, I damned a part of myself.*

J: *You can also bring balance to that by doing or being of service to other people. Do you think that would help you? If you offered your services and assisted other people?*

F: *I do not know anymore. I have stayed in this place, never venturing out but hoping an end would come to the anguish.*

J: *And it will. The things that you remember, that bring you pain, are memories. The way you are now and the way things are now, are so different, but you haven't noticed. What I want you to do right now is to look deep inside yourself at the very core of your being. Not at any particular event or time, the very core of your being and see if you can bring it up. What do you see?*

F: *I see a bright spot. I have always thought I was to hide here. I see a bright spot.*

J: *And as you watch it, what happens?*

F: *I see the truth. I see then, who I am. It is to say essence. That's who my son is.*

J: *Yes. It's the same essence that's in all of us. We call it the God-light. The white light. That's what connects us all. That's why it's so easy for me to talk to you. And why it's so easy for you to speak through my friend and I can hear you. The friend that I called to you, the friend who lost his life because of you, because of your actions, do you see that same life essence in him?*

F: *And more.*

J: *Move a bit closer to him and ask him if what I've said is true. If he chose that experience because he needed it for his spiritual growth and if in some way it was a gift you offered him.*

F: *There were many lives that he has lived since this time. I am [unintelligible] once again to learn together.*

J: *How do you feel about it? Is it something you'd like to do?*

F: *We both agreed to do this again and again as brothers. So, I see that now.*

J: *In knowing that, do you feel there's any reason for you to stay here now? To stay where you've been these years?*

F: *My faith [unintelligible]. I grew up, was a strong faith. They [unintelligible] loved [unintelligible] everything that I knew. It was for this reason I feared venturing out of this place I have hidden.*

J: *But your truth is what lies inside of you.*

F: *Yes.*

J: *Have you released the guilt, confusion and fear?*

F: [Unintelligible]

J: *Do you see the look of joy on your son's face as he watches this?*

F: *Yes.*

J: *Are you ready to go and return to the light? I'll ask for angelic protection for you as you return on your way…*

F: *Yes, yes, it's time.*

J: *Yes it is. Thank you for coming to talk with me. I appreciate your trusting me to help you with this work. It's been an honor for me.*

F: *And I. I could offer you the greatest of thanks and if I could ever help bring honor to you, who have honored me.*

J: *You have. You have honored me with your trust. It's very great of a gift.*

F: *I want to go on.*

J: *Thank you for coming to talk with us. Perhaps we'll meet again if you really choose to do the work of coming back and helping other souls who are trapped as you once were.*

F: *This would be a great honor.*

J: *St. Michael, I ask you to send angelic protection to guide this beautiful light being back to the light, and I send you on with blessings of peace and love. I call upon the healing angels to fill any voids created by the passing of this earthbound. And now we'd like this man's son to talk to us again.* [Long, long pause.] *I'm sure you remember his son was the person who told us his father was in a state of fear and confusion and was trapped here. I'd just like to see if he's willing to talk with us again, see how he feels about everything.* [Another long pause.]

Mr. P: *For a time. I will remain as a visitor. The work* [unintelligible] *now that my father has moved on to grow and has become even brighter. I may not appear as solidly as I did once.*

J: [Smiling.] *Well, that's ok because you already got her attention that way.*

Mr. P: *Our work together will span many years.*

J: *When you say "ours" do mean yours and Donna's?*

Mr. P: *Yes.*

D: *Does he want me to go back to the cemetery and try photographing?*

Mr. P: *You may.*

J: *Is there anything you would like for Donna specifically to focus on?*

Mr. P: *It would be a great pleasure for you to research our connection.*

D: *Can you lead me in any direction? Give me some names to start with.*

J: *Can you give Donna some names to start with or some kind of guidance so she will know where to begin? The name that you gave me before, was that a starting point?*

Mr. P: *Yes, Hiram was the name I was given when I arrived here. In the old country it was Helios.*

J: *Are you a brother of Philo, whose name was on the tombstone, but your name was not there? Because there were three names: a husband and wife and a son.*

Mr. P: *I go further ahead. I became a keeper of the books, many businesses in this and other cities.*

D: *Ask if he showed up in my kitchen.*

J: *Did you appear in Donna's kitchen?*

Mr. P: *Yes.*

D: *Should I start with Coudersport, Pennsylvania?*

Mr. P: *Start with the farm. Tobacco and horses; two locations.*

D: *Can you tell me those locations? Or give me some general idea?*

Mr. P: *Yes, to the west. Those farms were to the west. Tobacco farm was close to the shore and to the east of the river.*

D: *Is that information I already have regarding Peet property in Stratford?*

Mr. P: *Yes, that's one location.*

D: *Is there anyone I should be looking for that would help further the connection between the families?*

Mr. P: *None that live here.*

J: *The show is almost out of time, but I'm going to keep Paul under hypnosis so that Donna and Hiram may speak further. I'll close this show by saying that I will invite Hiram to come back whenever he chooses, if I can ever offer my assistance or he his, and welcome him that way. Obviously, Donna and I are going to be doing a lot more work together as it's only the beginning of a very nice connection for us, and I will also call Paul up from hypnosis and ask for any of his insights he may have seen while under. But before I call Paul up, I'll have him make sure he is completely filled with light and has a protective aura around him. Now a little bit previously, when I helped his father pass into the light, I asked that the healing angels to help fill any voids that may have been left. That's important because everything is energy, and there's a void created by the removal of an energy source and then any other energy could fill that place and we want to be sure it is filled with light. So, that's what that was about. I'm going to finish up by letting*

Donna and Hiram talk, literally until we run out of time. I thank you for watching The Sacred Journey *and thank you for your patience because technically I know this show has been very different from the others with all the things going on in the background, but I think that it was really interesting work that needed to be done.*

D: *Ok, Hiram, it's Donna, and I'd like you to give me a little more detail into my research into our past and family ancestry. I'd like to know if it was you who guided my hand in the library when I came upon the Peet family information?*

Mr. P: *Yes, but in establishing the locations, you will gain more information to continue with your search across the states.*

D: *Into Pennsylvania?*

Mr. P: *Yes.*

D: *Are aware of me when I drive by the cemetery and say "Hi"? Does it make you happy?*

Mr. P: *It has always brought joy knowing the work that you do.*

D: *Have you shown up in my photos of the cemetery in other forms? Are there other souls there?*

Mr. P: *There are other souls in that place…and guards.*

D: *Did you want to tell me something specific the night you showed up in my kitchen? Did you just want me to see you?*

Mr. P: *Our hearts and minds have spoken. It's a long journey and a difficult one to appear as that. And so distant a place as [unintelligible] our spirits alone, and I speak to your spirit at that time. The words that we have spoken will come to you in time…in a dream.*

D: *Will this help me in the research?*

Mr. P: *This will help you in your work of recording the spirits of those that remain and move from place to place on this earth.*

D: *Do you think I'll have more luck with, um, are you aware of me speaking with your descendant John Peet, when I got together with him, and I showed him the photo of you?*

Mr. P: *Yes.*

D: *Will he be of further help to me? Should I contact him again?*

Mr. P: *Yes.*

D: *Is there anything you want to tell me specifically?*

Mr. P: *Yes. It was you.*

D: *I don't understand.*

Mr. P: *It was you who were born as our younger sister. It was your spirit as her soul that came into this family and moved to the west.*

D: *What was the name?*

Mr. P: *Her name was kept from generation to generation. Her name was Phyllis. Philomena was the name at birth.*

D: *I'm confused.*

J: *Why don't we conclude, Paul shouldn't be under for much longer. Is there anything else, Hiram?*

Mr. P: *I'm finished at this time. My work here will continue. My work has come to a joyful end for my father.*

Joyce now brings Paul out of the hypnotic trance he has been in and reminds him to fill his body with white light and to be sure to have an aura of protection around himself.

I asked Paul about his impressions of these spirits and also about the transmission of information that had just gone on. He stated that there was rarely any dictation at all, but instead a steady influx of images and pictures, which were almost immediately comprehended and understood by him. He said that this would literally allow for an hour's worth of information to come through in a matter of minutes. Joyce stated that while she was conducting the session she was also present psychically and overseeing everything that went on.

To summarize and make a long story short, I have learned of a family connection with myself and the Peet family in a previous incarnation and that Mr. Peet foresaw the whole encounter from the time I stopped to take the photo to my meeting with Joyce St. Germaine, so that we would end up in the channeling session and he would find help for his father, who was earthbound by his own guilt due to murdering a friend in a drunken rage. He also appeared, he said, to help me further my work in the field of psychic photography and paranormal investigation (the photo has gone on to be voted one of the top ten ghost pictures of all time).

He has been seen in my home on at least two occasions and outside of my home at group functions and other places I happen to visit. He appeared to a police officer friend and Cosmic Society member and told her "Donna's my sister" while she was lying in bed. She had no knowledge of the information that had come through during the channeling session, and it was with much trepidation that she came forth and told me what had transpired. It only served to cement the validity of the whole experience to me.

As you can well imagine, I have much to do in the area of researching all of this information and substantiating it. I'm not disputing the above information, but I can see a few discrepancies right off the bat, such as when I asked if we were related and he said "distantly" but then further on in the session he claimed I was a younger sister (maybe he meant "distantly" as in from lives lived hundreds of years ago). Also, the original Peet family I've been researching came over from England and the descendants were born here in America. I can't make the connection with the name given as the father and also a "Hiram" or "Helios" Peet. There are other questions I have concerning the nature of the channeling itself, but I'm sure I have a lot to learn regarding all of these issues, and I certainly know I have a lot more "digging" to do before I uncover what all of this means and how it may all fit.

There have been other sightings of Mr. Peet by myself and on a few occasions by independent psychics, so I am sure that the person in the photo and the figure I have seen are one and the same. Then there are the many synchronistic events that led me to all of this in the first place. He has proclaimed that he "goes where I go" and is helping to keep me protected in my line of work; for this, and for all that he's done, I thank you, Mr. Peet. The rest, as they say, is history and is still unfolding—history that I need to research. The time line continues…

THE BOOTHE PARK MUSEUM, HOMESTEAD AND BURIAL GROUNDS, INCLUDING THE PECK'S MILL POND TRAGEDY

Rumored to be "the Oldest Homestead in America," the Boothe Park dwelling was built in Stratford, Connecticut, atop the 1663 foundation of the original abode in 1820. The first residence was constructed by Richard Boothe; originally from England, he was the first Stratford settler in the Boothe lineage and patriarch of one of the original forty founding families of Stratford. He is descended from William the Conqueror's right-hand man, the Norman knight Adam de Boothe. Generation after generation of the Boothe family were born, lived, worked and died at the thirty-two-acre estate they tended as farmland. A good number are remembered in marble monuments in the family graveyard that sits adjacent to the land. Most notable of the Boothe descendants were the park dwelling's last (and, in a way, current) occupants before it was willed to the town in 1949.

Mr. David Boothe Sr. was born here in 1813. He grew to be an active farmer and, later, an agent for a company called Adrian's Platt that bought, sold and repaired farm equipment and machinery. He was on the board of trustees of several banks in nearby Bridgeport. David was also heavily involved in the Congregational Church and was known for his Sunday sermons preached from his own yard's rock pulpit. He was said to be a very stern man in his religious convictions and staunch Christian dogmatic approach; this didn't bode well for his wife Betsy, whom he married in 1865.

Betsy was psychically gifted, and her husband believed that her intuitive "information" or her way of "just knowing" things before they would happen could only be the devil afoot. Thus, there were many occasions that

The Boothe Park Homestead.

her husband, being the good Christian man he thought himself to be, would "help" his wife find her way back to Jesus by "beating the devil out of her."

Betsy's life, while privileged financially and of a certain social status, was lived in heartache and sadness. She had been happily married, but her first husband, Rufus Beasley, was killed in the Civil War. Then both of her parents followed into the graveyard. In the same year still, her one-year-old infant died, and it was soon after that the devastated woman met and married the much older David Boothe, who would never understand her.

When the Boothe ancestors arrived in America from England, they quickly anglicized their name and dropped the *e* at the end. In 1865, in order to distinguish themselves apart from Lincoln's assassin, John Wilkes Booth, the family opted to add the letter back on.

Son David Jr. was born in 1867, and Stephen was born two years later in 1869 (right after the Civil War, and ironically, both died two years apart just after World War II).

David Jr. started going around the Northeast with his father and developed his love of travel and of other cultures and traditions. Referred to as "Mr. Outside," David was hardworking and skilled with machinery, tools and farming equipment. Stephen ("Mr. Inside") was more of a "mommy's boy," growing up and helped around the house doing cooking, needlework, crocheting and similar chores.

Mrs. Boothe's sons were the only bright lights in her life, but to the elder Boothe, his wife's encouragement of the boys to use their extrasensory perception, which she felt both were endowed with, was unconscionable.

The brothers remained farmers until the 1930s, when the industry shifted westward to some extent. Land was bought and sold, and at the time of their deaths they owned over one hundred rental properties in nearby Bridgeport on which they collected rental fees. Known as kind landlords, they were often lenient toward tenants who couldn't always come up with their lease payments due to hard economic times.

During the Christmas holiday season, they would often buy red mittens and candy for their boarders, knowing that they couldn't afford presents. One story speaks of David Jr., who wasn't as "polished" as his brother Stephen but was instead quite shabby and unkempt in appearance. David called upon an elderly tenant to collect the monthly fare, and the woman, eyeing his apparel, remarked, "Oh, Mr. Boothe, for such a big and important man in town, you really shouldn't look so scruffy!" He was missing a couple of buttons on his coat. She asked him inside so that she could sew new buttons on the jacket for him, which she did. She then said, "The next time you come and collect the rent I want you to go out and buy yourself a brand new suit. You have enough money to get one." Sure enough, the next month when he came around, he asked the woman "How do you like my new suit?" "Oh, dashing, Mr. Boothe!" she replied "You look wonderful and I am so glad you took my advice!" "Yes," he said, "I bought it at the Salvation Army for $1.50!"

The brothers were very generous with their money, but stories of this sort often left them misunderstood. One local market owner was paid $25 per month (about $400 today) so that David could have the privilege of helping himself to any produce he wanted from the store, often to onlookers' dismay. They would complain to the management that they'd seen him "swipe an apple" or other piece of fruit, and the store owner would reply "No, that's just Mr. Boothe; he can take whatever he wants!"

Physical proximity and an act of their generosity connect them to the Peck's Mill Pond and the new trolley line. The brothers sold portions of their land along the Housatonic River to the Bridgeport Traction Company in 1897 so the trolley line could be extended from Bridgeport north to Shelton. There was a large amusement park in Shelton that had attractions, rides and hot air balloons on Sundays. People would drive up by horse and buggy to see these sights; now the trolley would transport folks so they could witness the wonders of the area they were passing through.

The sale went into litigation because the brothers didn't want to lose their farmland in the process. They ended up having to cede the land and asked only for one-dollar remuneration on the deal. In return for their generosity, they were given free access and fare to anywhere the trolley went (normally a nickel fare) and bestowed with a barrel of trolley tokens, which they never used (they have since disappeared along with many other artifacts), but it was "just a given" that they could ride for free. However, to those who didn't know of all their behind-the-scenes wheeling and dealing, they appeared as cheapskates and were often misunderstood, particularly by people in the neighborhood, who could never seem to figure the two out. There are literally thousands of documents in the archives supporting their munificent gifts to people and lists of things that were freely given away; filing cabinets house a virtual paper trail of their benevolence, kindness and charitable giving.

On August 4, 1899, the governor of the state along with a few state senators and twenty-five people boarded the new ride and all was well. Nonetheless, two days later the site was scene of one of Connecticut's most catastrophic disasters.

Fed by the Pumpkin Ground Brook, Peck's Mill Pond is approximately one acre in size and had been a favorite fishing and hiking site and swimming (neighbors say skinny-dipping) hole for years.

The trip had started out normally that Sunday, and witnesses say they could see and hear the festive passengers singing as the trolley car went passed; some say it had been traveling at a higher-than-usual rate of speed. At some point on the steep incline, the car began to increasingly rock, and the songs turned into deathly screams. The car, unprotected by any guardrails, with its fresh new wheels, left the slick and barely used rails fifty-seven feet above the pond. The car careened downward on the ties for about seventy-five feet, when it bounced off the trestle and plunged into the pond below, overturning completely and landing on one end. When the car hit the mud below, the four-ton motor and the heavy trucks slammed into it, instantly crushing and killing thirty-six of the passengers. Two people jumped off to relative safety, merely breaking their bones. The remaining were seriously injured. Makeshift first-aid stations were commissioned of neighbors' houses, and Stratford's Town Hall improvised a morgue in its main lobby. Within a few hours, twenty-three corpses were laid out, awaiting identification, and town officials had their hands full implementing crowd control to the over one thousand people who arrived in hysterics at the possible thought of

The site of the Peck's Mill Pond tragedy.

their loved one's accidental demise. Six times as many showed up at the scene of the accident, which was described as pandemonium (complete with rampant pickpocketing). A speed limit of "not faster than four miles an hour" was immediately imposed, and business as usual resumed without further problems. To the psychically attuned, the area has an aura of disaster that, like some of its victims, remains to this day.

The Boothe Park Homestead site was listed on the National Register of Historic Places in 1985. Many renovations have occurred over the years. The renovation in 1913 by David and Stephen added stained-glass windows (red glass was priciest), four safes in the walls and several rubber puzzle-piece floors. Up until their deaths, the brothers obsessively collected buildings and other memorabilia from America's past.

The barn was built in 1880 and in 1913 was converted for use as the first museum building on the property and called the Anniversary Building in commemoration of 250 years of family on the site. In the same year, it was topped with a clock tower from a church in Massachusetts (which had been acquired by the entrepreneurial brothers in exchange for a Eureka

The Clocktower Building.

carpet sweeper), complete with an incredible Howard brand clock and Westminster chimes. There are five impressive, massive bells up in the cherry wood tower inscribed with the Boothe genealogy. A brass eagle is perched on top emblazoned with the numerals "1663–1913." Aside from going all the way to the railroad station in town to check the time (most people didn't even have pocket watches in those days), the clock chimes from the farm "gave everyone the time of day" quarterly and hourly; however, neighboring chicken owners initially complained, and the town imposed an evening noise ordinance to which the brothers responded by shutting the clock down at night and claiming they'd "no longer give Stratford the time of day." The brothers did, however, give the time of day and much more to the Native Americans, of whom they were predominantly fond and were in kind respected and honored by many tribes. There are volumes of letters between them and one Indian chief, Redwing, in particular, whose remarkable headdress is on display inside the clock tower building.

There have been numerous sightings of a hooded figure or that of a man in a top hat on the walkway of the tower. He has appeared holding a lantern and swinging it out in front of him as if to shoo people away. This same specter has been seen, again with a lantern, running from the caretaker's house to the old homestead. It was said that Stephen Boothe used to do just that at times to make the homestead appear "lived in."

In the 1970s, the Rosicrucian and other spiritualist groups held meetings in the homestead, and on one occasion they had a séance, intentionally summoning a dark entity, when suddenly almost all of the participants suffered pains in their heads and ran out to the front lawn vomiting; they claimed to have seen a man with a lantern outside. Shortly after this, meetings were barred from all groups inside the homestead.

In addition, the grounds boast a carriage house, used on the farm to house sleighs, carriages, carts and tack, some of which it still does. Oxen were yoked in here prior to heading out to pasture.

The Americana Museum building was the horse barn in the past and suffered a severe fire in May 1930 in which two other large barns were lost. All of the horses were saved, including one that was thirty-eight years old.

There is a miniature lighthouse (1919) that used to hold water and small-scaled boats. The brothers claimed that "this is the only lighthouse in America to which the government doesn't send supplies."

The current town garage on the property was built entirely of brownstone, offered free of charge to people courtesy of the National Trust Bank of Bridgeport, which was upgrading to a bigger and more modern structure.

Hoping to get rid of it cheaply, the bank's offer went unmet as no one was able to haul the huge blocks away. The Boothe brothers, however, arrived with stonecutters and halved the blocks, making them much easier to transport.

There is a miniature windmill that was rigged with over seven hundred Christmas lights on the sails and tail and then lit up during festivities and important events at the park.

The still operating blacksmith shop was built out of a rivalry with Henry Ford (who had built a large museum with a "smithy" in Deerfield, Massachusetts). In Bessie Burton's *The Friends of Boothe Park*, it was noted: "Well, Henry Ford built a Blacksmith shop with 4 sides and 4 corners, but we've built ours with 44 sides and 44 corners and that's not counting the east, west, north or south or the sunny side and of course there's not a shady side to anything the Boothe brothers do!" There are three spires on the top of the two-story redwood building that somehow align with the three massive crosses on the lawn that were built on the nearby hill in commemoration of their mother after she died.

Strangely impressive is the basilica, with its rock pulpit, which in 1938 hosted up to four thousand people attending Easter Sunday services, and all religious denominations were welcomed. Utilized during services were the three crosses, an antique organ and the chimes and bells that could be heard issuing from the clock tower. The sermon was followed by a fancy breakfast for all. David and Stephen went to Jerusalem and bought back a thorn tree, which was planted directly behind the middle cross to represent the one that Christ was crucified on.

The 1844 Putney Chapel was built to alleviate the four-mile drive into town to attend church services. Too many people happened to drive straight into it on Chapel Street, so it was moved nearby and across the road.

The 1930 one-of-a-kind Redwood Building is made completely of redwood; all the pieces are the same size, and they had been shipped east of the Mississippi, through the Panama Canal. All of the boards are laid flat sideways, and even the block windows are horizontal. It was dubbed "the Depression Building," and the brothers liked to joke that "the depression is like this building, flat broke and in the red." It now showcases many crystals, geodes and rare rocks, as well as an eclectic mix of stuffed, wild-eyed animals.

Opposite, top: The blacksmith building or "smithy."

Opposite, middle: The basilica with outdoor pulpit.

Opposite, bottom: The Redwood Building.

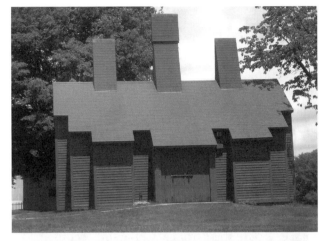

There's a "Coliseum/Hall" (relocated from the northeast corner of the farm and recycled from an old barn) at which the brothers would hold dinners and huge parties and is now rented out as a hall for similar occasions.

Also situated on the property are an icehouse, tollbooths (saved from demolition in 1988 when road tolls were banned in Connecticut), a trolley station, a planetarium (right next to the cemetery—symbolic of "above and below" or "heaven and earth") and an award-winning rose garden centered on an antique Boothe family fountain.

When the Friends of Boothe Park Association initially came into the project in 1984 and assessed the buildings and what needed fixing, it had no knowledge of any type of paranormal activity. Before long, however, according to Vice-President Bessie Burton, "At least four different individuals heard a woman calling to them from Mrs. Boothe's bedroom. They couldn't get in as the town had many of the rooms locked off." Upon approaching the doorway, the voice would stop. Noises and unexpected sounds were discerned that shouldn't be heard in an unoccupied house. Many people heard talking and laughing but could not make out what was being said. Cold spots and rushes of air with no particular source were felt. "Many people involved on the committee were psychically sensitive and able to pick up on these types of energies. The town workers became more and more aware of happenings in the house, too." Bessie said, "It wasn't a very comfortable place to work."

As progress began with organizing and categorizing the materials and house possessions, producing records, reading letters and learning about the family's lives, and as more and more of the antiques and pieces became restored, the tone seemed to change. It seemed that the right people came onboard, and with more and more positive events, things fell into place. But paranormal events of all kinds continued to happen, year after year, most likely a "ripple effect" of the "real world" atrocities that began to come to light.

It was in early June 2000 that another horrible tragedy was discovered, ironically enough, on a beautiful day at the park where a group of animal lovers had gathered for a dog show held on the grounds. At one point during the competition, someone noticed a bedraggled kitten in dire need of medical help and covered in feces exiting a window onto the roof of the 1920s Queen Anne–style Victorian home that was supposedly being used as a caretaker's residence. This home was initially built for park benefactor Stephen Boothe when his brother David got married. Workers were barely able to enter the building, as the stench of dead animals and feces—up to three inches thick

The award-winning rose garden. Note the radio wire towers in the background.

on the floors—overwhelmed them. Extensive damages in millions of dollars were the result in the building, and health officials declared the town-owned house unfit for occupancy.

It was during the scene of tending to the sick or euthanizing the dying felines that signs of devil worshipping were discovered in the attic. "Like attracts like" in the spirit world, and so it was in a warped way befitting that the "Black Altar"—a four-foot platform covered in barely visible red cloth, melted candle wax, inverted pentagrams and other signs of Satanic idolatry—was found literally covered with feces. At the base of the structure was a decaying German Shepherd that had been ritualistically tortured, lending more evidence of the occult practices that had been going on for some time in the attic area of the neglected estate. Nefarious parties and goings-on had been previously reported to town officials. It also lent more information on the lifestyle, mindsets and intentions of the family that had been appointed to be in charge of and in residence at the Boothe estate.

The town conducted an investigation into whether its policies were violated, and the police looked into whether there was any violation of the law. A $1,000 reward was offered for any information on the situation. The caretaker, who had not regularly been on the premises in accordance with

The Caretaker Building after multimillion-dollar renovations.

the conditions of his job, never faced any charges and was last known to have continued receiving a pension, making the situation rife with stories involving town coverups, payoffs, rip-offs and other questionable political monkey business at the city's government level. These questions have been left unanswered and unsettled but *not* forgotten by many a dismayed resident and, I'm sure, by town officials as well.

But money solves everything, right? After years of desertion, it was announced by the mayor's office that the park would receive a $200,000 grant courtesy of the Connecticut Commission on Culture and Tourism, and a matching sum provided by the town added another $200,000 into the restoration and cleanup project.

Boothe Park is a scheduled stop on many Haunted Connecticut tours, which lends to my being on the grounds most weekends during the end of September through mid-November for the Halloween season—the time of the summer solstice and when the veil between the worlds of the living and the dead is thinnest. It is believed that spirits have free will to roam the earth then. Due to the amount of buildings and sites on the property, a typical tour at the park with Haunted Connecticut will have the tourists divided into smaller groups and will sightsee with several docents at different intervals, switching locations occasionally in order to accommodate everyone being able to see all the attractions.

One such group happened to be upstairs in the former Civil War room at the homestead while another was traversing the parlor, kitchen and dining room on the first floor. Everyone at once heard a single, extremely loud bang or thump (much like a cannonball being slammed onto the wooden floor). It seemed to emanate from upstairs, and we actually looked for ceiling damage due to the forcefulness of the sound. The folks upstairs said it came from the room in which they were standing but that it had no logical source. Some guests were too frightened to continue the Boothe tour itinerary and headed back to the bus. At least ten different tour participants and countless young schoolchildren on field trips have complained of feeling ill upon entering the homestead (at different times and on different tours) and have had to be physically removed from the building.

Several teens volunteer their time as tour guides at the homestead and have experienced many things for themselves; one boy, who happens to have strong psychic tendencies, has had his hair pulled and been physically pushed around by an entity, scaring him away from volunteering for a while. This same boy had a dream of a cross being on the floor somewhere in the building. Weeks later, as furniture was being moved in the pantry, an inlaid cross was found hidden under a rug, embedded in the rubber floor, which is unique to the building.

During a recent Cosmic Society filming at the homestead for a seasonal news program, many paranormal activities happened just prior to our arrival; for instance the phone system went "wacky," ringing with no one on the line, followed by not working at all. Brand-new, fully charged video camera battery packs were completely drained on four separate cameras. Two professional TV show video recorders refused to operate; power was established, but with one, we could not get it to record, and the other, although completely connected, would not provide power. They worked fine, however, both before and after the attempt at the park.

One part of the show focused on a Cosmic Society member who was attempting an EVP session. She began by stating her name and intentions and then inquired if any spirits present would like to address the recorder. At that moment, three *loud* bangs sounded, caught on news cameras. They had never been heard before and have not been heard since that time. Several white orbs were videotaped, as well as captured on digital and 35mm cameras.

Minutes later we were in the attic and, after filming, took a quick break. Spotting an old and worn straw hat, I impulsively put it on my head and began goofing around and posing for a friend's camera. It was then that I had my own interaction with the spirit of Mr. Boothe, whom I later learned was the owner of the straw hat. We had taken two or three photos when suddenly I heard a very loud, very stern voice harshly yell "That's disrespectful!" so close to my ear that I could feel breath on it. Needless to say, I removed the hat and returned it to where I found it lickety-split.

Teenage sisters Chelsea and Jessica, also volunteer docents, were invited by Cosmic Society to join in on the TV program in order to relate their unique findings and personal observations, including one occasion of a doppelgänger. Jessica was talking with a small group of people and excused herself to go to another room. The kids remained where they were, talking. A moment later, "Jessica" walked past the group and into the dining room with attached pantry; as she did so, someone from the group asked her to grab a soda for him. Staring straight ahead and without acknowledging the request, "Jessica" strode into the dining room and turned the corner out of view. Just then the real Jessica walked out from another section of the dwelling. The startled group wondered how she could have accomplished this since the dining room/pantry had no other exit except the one she had just entered earlier. "Jess, where's my soda?" a friend asked. The real Jessica explained that she had never come back to this section of the house until just that moment and no idea what they were all talking about. Checking around, no other Jessica could be found.

Another volunteer who had become a Cosmic Society intern sent me this letter:

Hello Donna,

My name is Sarah Cohen and I'm a resident of Stratford, CT. I am a freshman at Bennington College in Vermont. Thank you for accepting my Field Work term application! I am excited to be an intern for Cosmic Society and working with you!

I am extremely interested in paranormal psychology, especially after having worked at The Boothe Memorial Park and Homestead in Stratford, CT, for three summers during high school. During this time I had many strange experiences including numerous sightings.

One time, while giving a tour of the building on a Saturday afternoon to an elderly lady, we stopped to rest for a minute in the kitchen. She and I were the only two people in the house and we suddenly heard loud footsteps as if someone was stomping on the floor. I could also hear what sounded like large heavy boxes being dragged across the floor, lifted and dropped back down again. I checked the room and found no one although the noises continued. A strong feeling to flee the house overtook me and both the old lady and I mutually left the building.

Then there was the incident that happened while up in Mrs. Boothe's bedroom alone. I turned to leave the room and switch the light off when, while my back was turned I heard the sound of what I can only describe as a full skirt swishing and scraping along the floor towards me. It scared me and I again left the house in a hurry.

On another occasion over the summer, I was guiding a tour for a mother and her two small children, when the little ones took off running toward the front staircase. I followed them to make sure they didn't get hurt or damage anything. I saw them run upstairs but when I started up the staircase myself, everything went completely quiet and I got a "cloudy" or dizzy feeling in my head. I saw what I can only describe as a cloudy blue mist going in and out of the office room upstairs. I was calm about it and didn't feel threatened or afraid. Within a few seconds the whole thing was over, my hearing returned and I saw that in fact the kids had not gone upstairs at all but out to the front porch.

I encountered this blue mist once more in the house that summer; I had shown up early for work but already it was too hot to wait outside. I let myself in through the kitchen and was alone in the house when the same phenomenon happened; I lost all sense of hearing and my mind went foggy. The mist appeared to come from the back hallway/staircase area and moved in and out of the doorway. Again this lasted only a few seconds and as the mist disappeared my hearing was restored. What is odd about this is that while it was happening I was completely calm, but as soon as I realized what had happened, I became frightened and had to leave the house.

I only once felt negative energy at the house. I had been on one of your tours and we were in the Putney Chapel. We started walking back towards the motor coach when I looked over at the front porch of the homestead and saw the black figure of a man pacing back and forth. I stopped dead in my tracks terrified and couldn't stop staring at him. I'm unsure why, but when I turned my head away I was filled with sadness and began to cry. No one walking along with me saw or experienced anything that I was aware of.

Thank you again Donna!

Sincerely, Sarah Cohen

Innumerable people, including many schoolchildren, have experienced an overwhelming sense of dread, temperature shifts, a feeling of being watched, dizziness, headaches and feeling physically sick to their stomachs in a particular room of the homestead. It was formerly known as the Civil War room—a small area where Civil War relics were kept. In an attempt to dispense the unstable energy, the room has since been converted into a nursery type of bedroom. But still the negative vibrations are discerned. Chairs have been situated just outside the doors of the room strictly for those who may need them after experiencing this room.

It was opening day in May 1985 when a Boothe relative was touring with a friend, looking over the exhibits and chatting. As soon as the friend stepped over the threshold of the Civil War room, she burst into tears. For no good reason she was overcome with sadness and grief. Her friend gathered her up and walked her out of the room to assist her. The second she stepped back out of the room, she returned to normal, and the two of them could not explain why that had just happened.

Many of the volunteers of Boothe Park and members of Cosmic Society have heard their names called, most often by a woman's voice, without there being a living human source. After turning off interior and exterior lights and exiting the building, volunteers would notice them on again within moments and also note emanations coming from sources that have no light sockets or outlets for lighting, especially in the basement, a place that continues to baffle paranormal investigators, as well as volunteers, security workers, tour guests and the unsuspecting public.

One night, Cosmic Society members and I were leaving the property after a photo shoot. Gary made a right-hand turn out of the driveway, and we needed to turn around. As we did so, lights in the upstairs offices came on and then went back out. We know that no one was inside the house. Prior to this, while taking photos, I saw movement in a downstairs window, and immediately following this we all witnessed a "white cloudy mass of energy" whoosh out from the window and straight at or through Gary. He immediately sensed a young girl in a white nightgown by an upper window of home and a man with a handlebar mustache. Bonnie snapped a few photos of the area the psychic was picking up on, although at the time she herself didn't see anything abnormal. While she was driving home, she had a dreadful feeling of someone else in the car, watching her. With trepidation she glanced in the rearview mirror and was horrified to see the upper torso of a man staring back at her from the rear seat of her car! It was an older man with an unmistakable handlebar mustache. Thankfully, he vanished and Bonnie said, "I couldn't drive home fast enough!" Having no idea what she had captured on her camera until after she could get the film developed, Bonnie was further shocked when she viewed two photos after processing; she had apparently captured a flesh-colored man's head with a handlebar mustache that had shifted position (moved from left to right) in the second-story window at which Gary had discerned the same specter.

On a recent tour, I was herding some of the group stragglers to board the motor coach and realized I was still missing a group of five. I ran back to the old house to find that three had come running just as fast to retrieve me! They had tried and tried for five minutes to get a basement door open that had been functioning perfectly minutes prior, and it refused to budge. At that point, a man said tauntingly, "Is there something in there you don't want us to see? Go ahead, open the door," which at that moment slowly creaked open on its own before their eyes. Not being seasoned investigators, this threw them into a tailspin as they never once thought it would actually *do* what was asked.

At another time, a small group of people posing as Cosmic Society members talked their way into the building for an investigation. Thinking that they were legitimate associates, Bessie Burton allowed them access to the building and left them alone to do what they wanted. Unfortunately, these phonies only ended up causing trouble to the extent that one member of the group got so frightened by the "spirits trying to get into her head" that she actually ran a few miles to a pay phone and called the police. Needless to say, they were asked to leave and never return to the property after it was discovered that they had no affiliation with our group.

An additional incident involved the finding of a secret room in the basement. Chelsea and Jessica and a few other school chums were looking over old blueprints of the property. They realized that there was a walled-up section in the basement that did not correspond to any of the prints, even the earliest originals. Excited, they decided to do some digging (literally) in the basement and first went to ask permission to remove a few bricks or stones from the strange room's outer wall. Getting the go-ahead, they headed for the cellar and were confronted at the top of the stairs by a most foul-smelling odor. They got a bit scared by it and decided to ditch their plans at unearthing the secret room. At that point, the smell slowly dissipated. It was later discovered that the wooden inlaid cross on the floor sits directly above this undisclosed area. A few days before our recent investigation on January 31, 2009, a "secret" door was discovered when a large piece of furniture was moved to paint behind it. The rectangular wooden panel on the floor, which had always been presumed to protect the wooden floor from marring, was actually discovered to be a door to a room in the basement, which was shown to have no foundation.

Then there is the Boothe family burial ground. Interestingly, Betsy isn't buried in the Boothe cemetery; she opted to be interred with her first husband elsewhere in Stratford. And although her physical body was laid to rest, Betsy's spirit has chosen to remain at the Boothe property in her postmortal state. Her apparition has been seen at least twice, by completely different people, at the top of the back staircase, looking down, wearing a long black dress with a white apron. Her restless soul acts as a guardian and protector of young children and those with psychic abilities who venture onto the property or attend one of many seasonal tours through the dwelling. Characteristically, her spirit energy is often sensed heavily and even photographed in her bedroom. It's a feminine room yet uncomfortable and claustrophobic. Hopefully, her spirit feels safe in it, but the vibe is of overwhelming sorrow and hopelessness.

A friend Rob and I were taking photos in the adjacent cemetery one evening, walking toward the back. Suddenly, and seemingly out of nowhere, I heard the sound of running water. At first Rob thought that I was imagining things, but seeing the look on my face and then hearing it himself proved otherwise. Following the sound, we found an antiquated hand pump gushing water! It took some effort for Rob to get it to shut off. It got very cold where we were standing, and after taking a few more photos, we left. Since that time, I have spoken with the niece of the caretaker of the Boothe estate, who told me, "That old pump hasn't worked for years!"

One other quite revealing event happened to Gary as he and I walked through the graveyard one evening in the 1990s. Upon reaching a certain tombstone, Gary felt stabbing pains in his back and actually fell to his knees on the ground in agony. This lasted for about a moment, and then we quickly left. Outside the iron gates, Gary returned to his normal composure. Later research determined that the site of the grave this occurred in front of was the site of a distant Boothe family member who died of a stabbing injury.

The Boothe Cemetery.

One previous caretaker, whose name will be withheld for obvious reasons, had been let go from his position at the park after charges of child molestation (on the grounds) surfaced; he was asked to leave town rather than face any trial or jail time. His disgusting acts were discovered after he and some other town workers, whom he supervised, raped a mentally challenged girl who lived just down the street. One woman, who as a child was one of his victims, is known to have been raped on the property and has spoken with Cosmic Society regarding her experience.

The second sordid caretaker, who through political ties was granted his position, became suspect as priceless pieces of Civil War artifacts began to disappear from the site. Four different journalists attempted to cover the story, but it was subsequently covered up instead. Not only were the details squelched, but those four writers were also each transferred to different jobs at different newspapers, and the scandalous stories were never made public.

Spending as much time as I and the Cosmic Society have done researching and investigating the Boothe Park Homestead, it has been concluded to have a high degree of paranormal activity with active poltergeist occurrences, ghost and apparition sightings and psychically impressed messages through radiotelethesis, thought transference, trance states and clairvoyant dreams of many individuals. The rare doppelgänger event is especially intriguing yet ominous. Some individuals have had bodily physical contact from an entity at the site.

The conditions for poltergeist activity at the location are highly prevalent; there is a balanced ratio of teenage energy in the building, as well as senior volunteers, mostly retirees. The land and property lend themselves to the paranormal conditions. In most instances, poltergeists are of a highly negative nature and are attracted to places that carry the vibrations of past acts and occurrences, using that energy in addition to usurping the environment, people and plants, etc., in order to manifest. Places where there are or have been sites of religious goings-on are usual targets. The hills of the park are adjacent to the river, which as paranormal investigators know contributes a high degree of energy and is conducive to psychic and paranormal phenomena. The grounds have been desecrated through immoral, illegal and unsavory acts including but certainly not limited to rape, illicit sex, drug use, robbery (of priceless Civil War artifacts), animal injury, cruelty and abuse, occultist conjuring, devil worshipping and satanic rituals. Add to this the family burial plot, high tension and radio transmission towers and the Peck's Mill tragedy property located within six-tenths of a mile, and you have many aspects that contribute to the unearthly goings-on here.

In most instances involving poltergeist energy, there is almost always the prevalence of earthbound spirits—especially with those of differing or opposing agendas. Poltergeist forces can usurp and at times manipulate or impress their will in order to control or dominate the earthbound soul(s).

Boothe Park Museum and the outlying buildings make for an interesting day trip for anyone interested in Americana, Stratford's early history, the Civil War and the life and times of the very bizarre Boothe family. Boothe Park at night, however, is a must-see, must-experience location for anyone interested in ghost hunting.

THE SHUBERT THEATRE AND
TAFT APARTMENTS

The Shubert Theatre, located at 247 College Street, New Haven, in the center of Yale University buildings, was originally built inside of a hotel, and guests had to make their way through the hotel lobby to actually reach it. It was also situated right next door to the famous Taft Hotel, now known as Taft Apartments, which has quite a history of its own and shares its many ghosts with the theatre.

The Taft began as an "ordinary" in the seventeenth century and then became Miles Tavern in 1690. Just after the Battle of Bunker Hill, George Washington stayed here in July 1775, when the building was known as Beers Tavern. In 1850, the site was demolished in order to build the New Haven Hotel. This closed to make way for the Taft Hotel, which opened on New Year's Day 1912. It was for eight years President William Howard Taft's home and workplace after his run in office and while president and law professor of Yale University. It housed numerous stars while their productions ran at the Shubert, and the theatre itself has been showcased in films including *All About Eve*, *Splendor in the Grass* and *Death of a Scoundrel*.

The Shubert brothers were theatrical managers and producers. They were Lee, Samuel and Jacob. All were born in the 1870s of an alcoholic father; the brothers were required to provide for the family as their patriarch should have but could not. It wasn't long before the three parlayed their mutually strong work ethics into the largest theatre empire of the twentieth century. Sam dealt with the creative aspects of the business, Lee was the production leader and Jacob dealt with shows in other areas of the state.

The Shubert Theatre.

The Taft Apartment Building.

Tragedy struck the trio when, on May 12, 1905, Sam was killed in a train wreck in Pennsylvania.

At that time in history, the brisk expansion of the Shubert Company was noticed by a group of producers and theatre owners known as the Syndicate. Abe Erlanger was the leader of this group, which literally controlled American theatre; it owned 75 percent of the playhouses in the nation, thus the majority of jobs in the field were under the direction of the Syndicate.

Lee Shubert was all set to sell out to the Syndicate, but Abel Erlanger misjudged the Shubert duo and their commitment to their fallen brother's memory when he offhandedly remarked that he would not honor or abide by any legal agreements "with a dead man." The insult to Sam's memory fueled a battle that would not end until the two brothers were victorious. They did this by playing on the sympathies of the vast population of workers in the industry and vowed to break the stronghold that the Syndicate had on them. The two were masters at manipulating publicity; their stance was, of course, well received by the press. Once, as they prepared a retirement tour for the venerated actress Sarah Bernhardt, the Syndicate closed them out of a city, and they were forced to retreat their production to canvas tents. Sympathizing with their predicament, the newspapers helped win even more support for the Shuberts with the county (in actuality, the brothers made much more money than they normally would have since the tents were significantly larger and accommodated many more seats than a theatre building).

Lee and Jacob named the New Haven playhouse in memory of their brother Sam, the founder of the Shubert empire. It was designed by New York architect Albert Swazey and built by H.E. Murdock in 1914. The Shubert Theatre was launched as a commercial venture because of its proximity to New York City, which is where the first Shubert Theatre was located. The New Haven Shubert allowed new shows to debut away from the glare of the press in New York; if the show was successful in New Haven, it would go on to Broadway. If again successful there, the show went on national tour.

The opening production was *The Belle of Bond Street*, and the price of seats ranged from $0.25 to $1.50.

Patrons were treated to a variety of plays, musicals, operas, dances, classical music recitals and concerts, vaudeville, jazz artists, big bands, burlesque and a variety of solo performances.

The musical *Robinson Crusoe Jr.*, starring Al Jolson, celebrated its worldwide debut on February 10, 1916.

Networks of Shubert theatres were built around the country, owned outright by the Shubert brothers until the 1940s. They had become the identical kind of controlling force they had once openly criticized. Antitrust laws forced them to divest themselves of most of those theatres, including New Haven, because they owned the product *and* its distribution. New Haven's Shubert was bought by Maurice H. Bailey in 1941. Today, none of the other early Shuberts is owned by the Shubert Organization, but the theatres still exist in Los Angeles, Pittsburgh, New York, Boston and Chicago.

Rogers and Hammerstein wrote a play entitled *Away We Go*, which had its world premiere at the Shubert New Haven. While rehearsing and reviewing the show, they decided it needed something lively and up-tempo, with the whole cast onstage. They retired next door to the Taft Hotel, where they proceeded to write the song "Oklahoma" in a single evening. Cast and crew alike loved it so much that the production itself was renamed *Oklahoma*. It went on to Boston still as *Away We Go*. However, the press agent from Massachusetts called New York and advised them to "throw away all of the 'Away We Go' posters and flyers with that name and reprint new ones with 'Oklahoma' on them." Fifty thousand full-color advertisements were printed and again thrown out due to the lack of an exclamation point after the word "Oklahoma," and yet another fifty thousand were printed to their liking. In 1945, *Oklahoma!* ran opposite *Carousel* (which also premiered at Shubert New Haven) on Broadway, New York, for many years.

Rogers and Hammerstein decided that the New Haven Shubert was their "lucky theatre." In 1945, they wrote *South Pacific* and *The King & I*, among others. All the new musicals had their world premieres at the Shubert New Haven, including the productions *Brigadoon*, *Damn Yankees*, *My Fair Lady* and *Annie Get Your Gun*, in addition to plays by Tennessee Williams, Arthur Miller and others.

Because of the many plays that have run here, the list of actors that have performed at the Shubert are a veritable who's who of American theatre. Marlon Brando had his stage debut here in *A Streetcar Named Desire*. The impressive list of actors who have made the Shubert a place in their hearts includes (but is certainly not limited to) the late Paul Newman, his wife Joanne Woodward, Humphrey Bogart, Audrey Hepburn, Kathryn Hepburn, the Marx brothers, Jimmy Stewart, Eve Arden, Tommy Tune, Marie Osmond and Stephanie Mills, among the many British and other actors who starred at the Shubert in other plays.

Gone with the Wind's lead actors and actresses graced the stage of the Shubert. Clark Gable (Rhett Butler) appeared in the world premiere of *Machinal* (September 3, 1928) and *Hawk Island* (September 1929). Vivien Leigh (Scarlett O'Hara) was at the Shubert in the American premiere of

Duel of Angels (April 3, 1960) and in Chekhov's *Ivanov* with John Gielgud (February 1966). Olivia de Havilland (Melanie) appeared with Henry Fonda in *A Gift of Time* (January 1962). Leslie Howard (Ashley Wilkes) played in John Galsworthy's *Escape* (April 1928) and in the American premiere of *Berkeley Square* (October 1929). Evelyn Keyes (Scarlett's sister Sue Ellen) starred with Don Ameche in the musical *No, No, Nanette* (December 1972).

Following suit, some lead cast members from *The Wizard of Oz* also appeared here. Bert Lahr (Cowardly Lion) entertained Shubert audiences for thirty-five years. His shows included *Harry Delmar's Revels* (November 1927); the world premiere of *Flying High* with Kate Smith (February 17, 1930); the world premiere of Cole Porter's *Dubarry Was A Lady* with Ethel Merman and Betty Grable (November 9, 1939); *Two On the Aisle* (June 1951); and *The Beauty Part* with Larry Hagman (November 1962). Frank Morgan (the Wizard) made his first appearance in the world premiere of Jerome Kern's *Rock-a-Bye Baby* (April 8, 1918). He returned in *The Dagger* (September 1925). Margaret Hamilton (the Wicked Witch) was in *The Men We Marry* (December 1947) and *Fancy Meeting You Again* (November 1951). Billie Burke (Glinda the Good Witch of the North) appeared in *Family Affairs* (December 1929).

The Shubert remained a viable commercial theatre until 1976, when the theatre closed down and was threatened with destruction. During those closed years, the surrounding neighborhood—which had been dependent on the theatre patronage—became a ghost town. Restaurants and shops were boarded up and abandoned as their businesses literally died off. The Taft also closed three years earlier and remained vacant for many years.

In 1983, it was purchased by the Columbus Association for the Performing Arts (CAPA) and refurbished by the Fusco Corporation. It reopened as a nonprofit performing arts center and now presents classical music, opera, dance, cabaret, ballet and more. Louis Armstrong performed on solo horn in the Shubert's orchestra pit. Appropriately, the very first show of the renovated theatre was entitled *While the Shubert Slept* and contained performances that may have very well had their premieres there instead of on the Great White Way. The Shubert's legacy of hosting premieres before their Broadway runs was back in action, with *Jekyll and Hyde*, Neil Simon's *Proposals*, *Stomp!* and *Civil War* (which had so much lighting equipment that much of it was left behind and is still being used by the Shubert). Recently, runs of *Tom Sawyer* and *Annie Get Your Gun* were performed. The theatre is also available for private functions such as parties and dance recitals.

But is the Shubert *really* haunted? This was the question members of Cosmic Society were determined to find out on July 17, 2000.

Roving reporter Anna Sava, for one of Connecticut's TV news programs (WTNH-8), was sent to explore the famous theatre in the fall of 1999. During the half-hour live episode, Sava, along with meteorologist Jeff Fox and a "psychic," Mark Salem, were shown "astounding" feats supposedly attributed to the Shubert's resident "ghosts." While Salem placed a piece of chalk between two small chalkboards, fastening them with rubber bands, Jeff Fox was ordered to randomly open a book. Mark asked Jeff to focus on the first few words at the top of the page. Laughingly, Fox stated the words "and friends." Salem then told everyone to concentrate while Anna Sava held the chalkboards. A moment later, the chalkboards were revealed to show the names of the building's previous owners, as well as the two words randomly found in the book by Jeff Fox: "and friends."

Next, Salem placed a clear crystal bell on a stool. He shouted out loud at the empty theatre, asking if anyone was present, and if so, to ring the bell. The studio camera then slowly focused on the bell and recorded the bell clacker slowly rock back and forth until it eventually rang the crystal bell.

Lastly, Mark Salem wanted to receive "voices from beyond" or Electronic Voice Phenomena (EVPs). To demonstrate that his recording equipment was working properly, he placed a prerecorded tape into his machine. Miss Sava was asked to direct her energy onto an unopened, brand-new audiotape. She was to envision the theatre's specters imprinting their disembodied voices on to the audiotape. After a couple of minutes, they unwrapped the packaging and put the new tape into the recorder. When they pressed play there was a definite EVP. Visibly shaken, Anna Sava insisted the machine be turned off, refusing to hear if anything further had developed.

The viewers were then clued in to the truth that Mark Salem was, in fact, a talented stage magician and mind reader; he admitted that the astonishing "evidence" had all been sleight of hand. He did *not*, however, like any magician worth his salt, reveal how the tricks had been carried out.

There were other stories about the Shubert, stories that didn't involve tricks or tricksters but were accounts of suicide, failed careers and lost hopes, "amazing" and "unreal" all the same. It was time we had a look for ourselves.

Due to nighttime performances, we had to schedule a daytime trip, which, you may be surprised to learn, is actually a very good time to do investigative research on alleged haunted properties. For starters, I always advise scouting out a potential site for any physical terrain issues or building flaws, structurally, mechanically or otherwise. From underground aquifers to radio towers, there are internal and external factors that can often emulate haunting phenomena. If you do have any paranormal happenings or experiences during the daylight that can be backed up with any type of tangible evidence such as EVPs, photos or video recordings, you're almost guaranteed to be on to something. I've learned in my experience over the years that most areas that show signs of daytime hauntings *do* have spirits in residence that are not always ghosts; these other types of entities are usually more powerful than an earthbound one and sometimes feature an unusually negative nature.

Theatres, for their own unique reasons, have a higher-than-average chance of being haunted. Not only does lighting play a huge part in any onstage production, but also in the arena of perpetuating and providing conducive conditions for paranormal phenomena to occur, being that theatres are most often darkly lit places that will absorb energy inward. The stage is bright and lit and gives off energy outward to those in the audience and the furniture and walls itself. This creates a kinetic flow of energy that can lock in on the people sitting there, compounding and harnessing the power of their thought energy that is occurring on a creative level. Altered states of consciousness can occur because of the imagery from the performance. A collective mind system and communal energy clusters in the space and leaves an impression or imprint. Spirits, which have mundane existences, go to a place of fantasy with which they can identify while caught between worlds. There is usually a story of a stagehand or actor, long dead, roaming the old-time theatres and movie houses.

Prior to a small crew of three Cosmic Society members (Alicia, Laura and me) making our way to the theatre that day, I did the usual background check on the location's property history, starting with the city overall, and learned that New Haven ("Elm City") was the most important manufacturing center in Connecticut for a brief period of time at the start of the twentieth century. There were close to five hundred manufacturers producing everything from hardware, ammunition and firearms to carriages, wagons, liquor and undergarments. (Sounds like a party town to me!)

Walking through the modern glass doors of the newly renovated theatre, the first thing we notice is the red carpeted staircase directly in front. From the ceiling and upper lobby area, large sparkling star "cut-outs" hang majestically. I am drawn to this area immediately, but unfortunately we aren't able to go upstairs. A ticket window sits to the left of the main floor lobby, and to the right a small concession stand (popcorn is no longer allowed) and boutique seem ready to serve visitors.

We are greeted by three staff members, Margo, Catherine and Doug, whose love of theatre, art and obviously the Shubert itself is most evident. They immediately state that they have never experienced anything ghostly in the theatre themselves but that they are "open to the possibility" of a haunting, and all had heard stories from staff and maintenance personnel.

Behind the stairwell and straight ahead is a large wall containing "The Board," a visual archive of many of the performances that have graced the stage of this historic landmark. It is the Shubert's own wall of fame (although there are numerous "walls of fame," as we are to see later).

Many shows, plays and performances, although not all, were recorded on "The Board" in the first run of the theatre (although if a show bombed, it rarely made it to "The Board"). A star rating system was used to identify the success of the shows, with three stars indicating a national tour and four denoting a "World Premiere!"

Standing on the tongue-and-groove wooden stage of the three-thousand-seat theatre is one of the most exciting moments of the day for me. Just knowing that all the famous actors, musicians and dancers have performed right here was thrilling! As I look out into the rows of seats (all reupholstered and designed to replicate the original seats—it actually looks most like it originally did in 1914), I immediately spot my exact seat from my attendance of *The Wiz* back in 1992. It is truly an incredible experience.

Some of the original theatre seats are still being used in the lower lobby. Two others are at the Rogers and Hammerstein Foundation in New York. A sale of the seats was made to public and private contributors of the Shubert, and others were given to nonprofit organizations, churches, schools, synagogues and Shubert staff.

The staff demonstrates the new speaker system, which accommodates about thirty people per speaker and is set up so that wherever one sits, the speaker is precisely timed to the millisecond—eliminating any sound delay for the listener. No matter where audience members are seated in the theatre, they will hear each sound synchronized at exactly the moment it is being performed onstage.

The actors love the intimacy that can be shared with the audience at the Shubert—such as making eye contact with those in the last row of the balcony. The only actor to perform there for five years *without a sound system* was Christopher Plummer in *Barrymore*, who commented, "It's about time I'm on a proper stage in a proper theatre!"

Because of its relatively small size, the theatre cannot properly host enormous productions such as *Phantom of the Opera* or *Miss Saigon*. It doesn't have the space, the stage or the access to get the equipment in.

Painting has restored the original design of the walls, with particular care and attention given to historical accuracy. Ivory, ecru and gold leaf (the original 1914 colors) were used in refurbishing the auditorium, mezzanine and balcony areas that had faded with time. The curtains and drapes, which had been literally ripped off by neighboring Yale students, were made into parts of the box seats on the sides to avoid further vandalism.

The orchestra pit is a bit intimidating. It is a long drop down from the edge of the stage. As I look at the pit from the vantage point of the stage, I am told the story of at least one actress who walked too far and fell. She was caught safely by the musicians below and received a huge round of applause. At the end of the night, she told her manager she wanted to repeat the act and was responded to with "Absolutely *not!*"

I notice the "ghost light," which stands solo onstage. The iron pole looks lonely and stark against the glare from a single, regular one-hundred-watt light bulb on the upper end. Most theatres have a ghost light for two reasons: if there are any spirits present, they will not feel alone, and secondly, so that anyone walking onstage in the dark (janitors or other workers) can see the edge of the stage to avoid dropping into the orchestra pit and perhaps becoming a ghostly resident of the place themselves.

Backstage, the original hemp pulley system—used to move backdrops, props and scenery—is still in place, although the ropes are changed periodically. The lights are all fastened on to pipes and are also raised and lowered using the pulley system. Some of the bricks behind the piping have graffiti from 1914.

We make our way down to the basement, which contains four "star" dressing rooms, each with a sitting room, shower and private bath. There are two "featured player" dressing rooms, as well as four larger "chorus" dressing rooms, which accommodate forty-four people and are used for changing, wigs and make-up. Additionally, laundry facilities stand on-site to clean players' costumes. We see a massive system of support beams that are used to raise and lower the stage above if it becomes warped. The dark wooden ceiling beams are 1914 originals from the building. Unfortunately, this portion of the building is not handicapped-accessible because it was grandfathered in (allowed to remain open only because it was built before the present system of eighty-eight fire codes a building must pass was put into place). The tongue-and-groove stage style is no longer built, as it is not up to code, but we are told that dancers love the extraordinary spring in the floor during performances.

One of many "graffiti walls" in the basement of the Shubert Theatre.

Energy exudes from the "graffiti walls." Every company that performs here has the opportunity to paint a space on the wall with the show's logo or artwork. Usually someone from the company does the actual work; however, a local artist is recommended if needed. Every member of the company signs the wall, and what a collection the Shubert has! *Man of La Mancha* was signed by Robert Goulet, *Damn Yankees* by Jerry Lewis, Neil Simon's signature is on *Proposals*, Christine Andreas and John Neville from *A Chorus Line*, Kirk Douglas in *One Flew Over the Cuckoo's Nest*, Mickey Rooney in *A Funny Thing Happened On My Way to the Met*, Julie Andrews in *The King & I*, Mary Martin in *The Sound of Music*, Michael Feinstein, Ben Stiller, Shirley Jones, Bernadette Peters and Cathy Rigby in *Peter Pan*...the list goes on.

The *Dial M for Murder* space is complete with a nonworking pay telephone; however, "someone keeps ripping off the scissors that belong stuck into the artwork." Supposedly, this is the poster that the cast signed, and the bloodstained portion feels wet if you touch it. The rest of the poster is dry. Interestingly, it was not designed that way. Companies such as the New York City Ballet are also offered space on the walls, and one dance troupe (I won't tell who!) actually used impressions of someone's "butts and breasts" in their space.

As we approach the lobby during our brief investigation, near the end of our stay, the staff reiterates an incident involving Marie Osmond. Apparently, where now hang the large cut-out stars, there were previously hung large caricatures of performers who had "worked the stage." As the story goes, Marie Osmond, who was doing a two-week run in *The Sound of Music*, walked through the lobby, and the large Mary Martin caricature started swinging for no explainable reason. There were no drafts, no air conditioning vents and no other caricatures moving at all. It swung for the entire two-week run. At the exact moment Marie Osmond packed her make-up kit and left the theatre, the caricature stopped swinging and hung calmly again with the others. Instead of being spooked by the affair, Marie took it as a blessing—an approval of sorts. The caricature is now on the wall in one of the staff offices.

When I bring up the subject of past deaths in the theatre, the staff tells of an Academy Award–nominated theatre actress and Hollywood star from the 1930s: Margaret Brooke Sullavan, born on May 16, 1911, in Norfolk, Virginia. She was the daughter of Cornelius Sullavan, a prosperous stockbroker, and his wife Garland Brooke. Miss Sullavan attended Chatham Episcopal Institute (now Chatham Hall), an all-girls college preparatory boarding school, becoming the student body president and delivering the salutary oration in 1927.

Relocating to Boston, she became a member of the Harvard Dramatic Club. She debuted in the undergraduate musical *Close Up* in 1929, where she met cast mate Henry Fonda. They married on Christmas Day 1931 (the same year she made her Broadway debut) but barely made it past Valentine's Day 1932 before divorcing; however, they remained friends for life.

In 1931, she was cast by Lee Shubert in her Broadway debut, *A Modern Virgin*, which initiated her friendship with the brothers. At the meeting, due to a cold, her voice was coarser than usual and Mr. Shubert took to it immediately, and Margaret proclaimed to continue it by "standing in every available draft."

Margaret arrived in Hollywood in 1933 on her twenty-fourth birthday. Her film introduction came that same year in *Only Yesterday*. She costarred in four films with James Stewart, who would later become a part-time babysitter to Margaret's future children.

She dated Humphrey Bogart but ended up marrying (her third husband) the father of her three children in 1936, Leland Hayward, who was an influential and wealthy talent agent and theatrical producer. In 1937, daughter Brooke was born, followed two years later by Bridget and an Oscar nomination. William arrived in 1941.

The children had what seemed an idyllic, fairy tale childhood. Their playmates and best friends included the offspring of Ingrid Bergman, Laurence Olivier, ex-husband Henry Fonda and Gary Cooper. In order for them to have a "normal" childhood and to isolate them from "the evils of Hollywood," Sullavan made sure they had everything at their disposal: a house of their own apart from their parents' in which they had servants, tutors and nannies; chauffeured shopping trips; and thrill rides in daddy's private plane. Holidays and birthday parties were spectacularly enviable social bashes. However, this lifestyle of the super rich and powerful played out like a Greek tragedy in the end. Their generational family misfortunes mirrored many in the lives of Eugene O'Neill and his clan with drug abuse, alcoholism, parental abandonment, selfishness and multiple suicides. (See my book *Ghost Stories and Legends of Eastern Connecticut: Lore, Mysteries and Secrets Revealed* for full story of the O'Neill saga.)

In the 1940s, Margaret went into semiretirement in order to perpetuate her idea of "normal" life. Unfortunately, the wiles of Pamela Digby Churchill (whose first husband was the son of former English prime minister Winston Churchill), who was famous for ensnaring wealthy husbands away from friends and foes alike, was too much for her husband to resist. Margaret sought a divorce and moved to Connecticut. Pamela and Leland then married, making the three Hayward siblings stepchildren to Pamela, who was reported to dislike them openly and served as a classic wicked stepmother. Despite this, Bridget and Bill dealt a crushing blow to their mother's fragile ego by opting not to remain with her but instead wished to live with their father. Churchill later became the U.S. ambassador to France. Leland went on to be married a total of five times.

While daughter Brooke was an attendant of Vassar and Yale and made strides as an actress, her brother and sister were both patients in mental asylums: Bridget, suffering from extreme middle child syndrome, the failure to live up to parental expectations and mental illness, at Austen Riggs in Stockbridge, Massachusetts, and Bill at Menninger's in Topeka, Kansas.

In 1950, Margaret married Kenneth Wagg, an English investment banker, and with high hopes came out of retirement in 1952 to appear in *The Deep Blue Sea* on Broadway. Her last onstage performance was *Janus* in 1955 at

New York City's Plymouth Theatre—which happened to be Shubert-built and Shubert-owned.

She had come to the Shubert to make a comeback, but grief and melancholy got the better of her. Margaret had a congenital hearing defect in her left ear called otosclerosis, which worsened with age and likely spread to the right ear. Her once beautiful looks and health, like her career, were careening downhill, furthering her depression. She was hopelessly troubled about her children's mental and emotional conditions and was quoted as saying:

> *Most actors are basically neurotic people; terribly, terribly unhappy. That's one of the reasons they become actors. Nobody well adjusted would ever want to expose him or herself to a large group of strangers. Think of it. Insanity! Generally, by their very nature—that is if they're at all dedicated—actors do not make good parents. They are altogether egotistical and selfish. The better the actor—and I hate to say it, the bigger the star—why, the more that seems to be true. Honestly, I don't think I've ever known one—not one—star who was successfully able to combine a career and family life!*

Despondent, she overdosed on barbiturates on New Year's Day 1960 next door at the Taft Hotel. Her tortured soul has been seen meandering around both of the locations; her negative emotions and grief keep her tethered to the earthly plane and to the last place she had sought her stardom. She eventually received a star on the Hollywood Walk of Fame.

Her daughter, Bridget Hayward, took her own life just nine months after her mother and in the same fashion—overdose by pills. She was found in her New York City apartment a month later. She was merely twenty-one.

William was an associate producer of *Easy Rider* in 1969, which helped fuel his love of motorcycles. In 1980, he produced his sister Brooke's bestselling 1977 exposé of the family's demons *Haywire* into a TV movie (also like O'Neill's family misfortunes penned in *A Long Day's Journey into Night*). He had a severe motorcycle accident in 2003 that left him gravely immobilized and mentally weakened. He was sixty-six when he shot himself in the heart with a handgun on March 9, 2008, in his trailer in California.

Back at the Shubert, we hear a report of a crew member who had died backstage. Alicia, one of my companions, senses "someone" on the left side of the stage. It is poignantly noticeable that our three guides are close-lipped with any details; however, they refer us to current crew members, many of whom have worked in the theatre for three or four generations. Inconveniently, the only crew member we see vanishes as quickly as he had appeared while we were onstage taking photos and hooking up equipment, cameras and meters.

However, reports and letters from present-day workers at the theatre continue to cross my desk, like this one:

> *Hello Donna,*
>
> *I am interested in getting and sharing a story about something that happened today to me in the basement of the Shubert Theater in New Haven. I can't seem to find any info on the history of the building. I'm a contractor and have been in just about every nook and cranny of the place but after today I might not set a foot in the building again. Could you please help me with some info on what is going on here? Thank you.*

And here was my reply:

> *Hi!*
> *Please tell me what happened, it sounds serious… Thank you for writing,*
> *Donna*

Here is his second letter:

> *Hello my name is Ramon Antonio Jr. I was in the lower boiler room when the cleaning lady told me that there was smoke coming from one of my units on the other end of basement. This is located directly under the stairs that were blocked off during the renovation in the early 80s. I turned off the unit but still saw smoke. It was coming from a garbage can next to the a/c unit. I looked in the can and find 2 pieces of paper towels and an empty bottle of cleaner, and the paper towels were smoldering. I then reached in to take out the paper and it burst into flames. We looked into the can to see if there was a cigarette or match and found none. Also the plastic bag did not melt or catch fire. I went back to the other side to finish what I was doing when a motor in the room started to make a noise that it shouldn't make unless it is broken. The other mechanic I was with looked at it and found no problems. It kept happening on and off for about 2 minutes and then stopped. He then walks over to me and asks me if I had taken anything out of my tool bag. I had not so he tells me never mind. I press him until he tells me and*

he says that my flashlight was on so he turned it off. This is when I got scared because on Tuesday I dropped my light off a ladder and broke it and there were no batteries in it. He then hits the button and it turns on. He hits it one more time and it turns off but then starts to flash on and off until I grabbed it and threw it on the floor. I've worked in the building since 2005 and always had a bad feeling about the place. This is just what happened today. This time last year I was almost hit by a car right out front. Then there was the time I was working on the roof and something or someone kept telling me to go to the top roof and check for a person. I found a man living on the roof. He had an axe and butcher knife with him when the cops searched his belongings.

Feel free to call me at anytime.
Ramon

Due to time constraints, we aren't able to stay for long, but our time there was worth every minute. The old historic theatre building has stood the test of time, most likely with the loving concern from spirits that watch over it, both here in the physical and those who still long to be. I leave the Shubert Theatre with a deep sense of connection to its history and its incredible contribution to the arts and show business in the United States.

UNION CEMETERY, SPORT HILL ROAD, OUR LADY OF THE ROSARY CHAPEL AND THE STEPNEY BURIAL GROUNDS, INCLUDING THE WHITE LADY

E aston, Connecticut, hasn't changed much over the years; traditional farmhouses and horse stables are commonplace here as well as 7,500 acres of wooded open space watershed and clear reservoirs. Although seemingly remote and definitely rural, the majority of dwellings and those maintaining them have a natural sophistication and a way about them that enriches the pristine New England countryside.

The communities of Easton, Redding and Weston were once combined and known as Norfield. Redding, as it would become, was known as the "oblong," the "peculiar" and the "common lands"—a two- by seven-mile stretch of land that was unclaimed by surrounding towns. All three towns were acquired as part of the Northern Purchase from local Native Americans on January 19, 1671, for "36 pounds sterling of cloth valued at 10 shillings a yard" (about seventy-two yards of cloth). Redding was settled in 1642 and became a parish in 1729. Easton itself, first settled in 1639, did not become populated enough for town status until 1845. Farming, milling and tanning were the mainstay employment avenues along with blacksmithing, ironwork and boot, shoe, button and comb shops.

Life wasn't easy, and injurious or deadly catastrophes and fires happened regularly in and out of the mills, barns and shops. Many died from fire injuries or through smoke inhalation, others lost limbs or digits to crude equipment and machinery and some even had their necks snapped as their hair caught up in the exposed leather belting that connected the ceiling-mounted drive shafts to such machines. Even with such hardships,

Union Cemetery's iron fence. Iron has been considered as a substance that can contain ghosts and spirits. Union's centuries-old fence appears to be a bit worse for wear.

Eastonites' attitudes toward refinement, affluence and education were advanced for their time, and the town continues to host residences for notorieties throughout the ages such as Mark Twain, Helen Keller, Hume Cronyn and the late Jessica Tandy.

As is typical in researching a haunted location, one usually starts with the property—the site itself and the surrounding area and land use. Sometimes you'll find that certain areas have a higher concentration for accidents, tragedies or failures, which of course could all be reasons for a spirit to remain earthbound.

Research points to Union Cemetery and the Easton Baptist Church being situated in just such an area. One can only surmise why that locale was originally known as Poverty Hollow. Why did the earliest settlers name the area the "peculiar?"

We focus on a stretch of land that encompasses two churchyards and two burial grounds, both infamous in their own rights and both linked by a specter that has been repeatedly seen and documented for several decades at both locations.

We begin at the junction of Sport Hill Road (Route 59, which bears right to become Stepney Road) and Westport Road (Route 136) and expand outward from the triangular patch of land known as Union Cemetery that

has attracted attention and visitors from all over the world. The area has been examined and studied well and well before we arrive at the entrance to New England's most haunted graveyard.

At a time when horseback riding gave way to horse and carriages, this juncture has been known as a deadly crossway. Here for many years was a rotary, and there were on too many occasions more and more vehicle accidents and disasters, until one particularly brutal fatality in the 1950s. It was then that the state commenced to rebuild the intersection.

Sport Hill Road (Route 59) actually got its name because of

The Easton Baptist Church.

the high-speed auto chases that took place annually at the last weekend of May 1906–1911. At the summit of the road and to the south, the starting line began at the Mill River Bridge, which also delineated the Easton/ Fairfield boundaries. The finish line to the north was marked at Flat Rock Road. One year, the winner's speed was clocked at an amazing one minute and seventeen seconds. In 1908, the event, sponsored by the Bridgeport Hydraulic Company, was attended by over ten thousand curious onlookers, making it one of the year's largest motor sport events. High technology of the day included stringing telephone line along the route, marking out ten equidistant speakers or "listening stations" that would project audible progressions of the cars and the race to the spectators even though the cars had long whizzed past them.

Just after World War II, the infamous road was rerouted to the east by the State of Connecticut after a terrible crash claimed the life of an unnamed victim—probably how Route 59 became "secret route 402" in the early 1940s. Secret routes are state-maintained roads that are not publicly numbered or signposted. It was also at the base of the hill where, for many years, folks observed a large, blue, five-pointed star that was lit in remembrance of the victims whose lives were claimed on Sport Hill Road.

Heading past the finish line of the Sport Hill races farther north, we uncover the site where, on February 16, 1779, prisoners Edward Jones, a spy, and John Smith, a deserter, were executed on Gallows Hill, located on Rock House Road east of the intersection with Sport Hill. Jones was hung, and he swung while Smith faced a firing squad. While actually part of Redding, Gallows Hill was located just under three and a half miles north of Union Cemetery.

As towns, they share a high school and land boundary—and a nightmarish crime. It was Valentine's Day 1980 when cheerleader Cara Quinn missed her bus to school. Hoping to catch a ride to Joel Barlow High School (in Regional District #9, which is a school to both Easton and Redding residents) before the late bell, she hitchhiked up Sport Hill Road. She was indeed picked up but never made it to her classes. The ride ended, as did her life, in Shelton, Connecticut. Cara was repeatedly raped before she was shot through the head and neck. It was a busy day for Martin Schifflett, a thirty-two-year-old career criminal, rapist and Cara's murderer, who still found time that afternoon to borrow money to buy his wife a couple boxes of candy and a card for the lover's holiday. A week later, he raped additional women in Bridgeport and Fairfield. Search teams of every age group were employed to scour the surrounding areas. Unusually placed shell casings led investigators

Left: The Our Lady of the Rosary Chapel. Notice the classic statue of the archangel Michael defeating Satan. This building is rumored to host the most exorcisms in the United States.

Below: Entrance to Stepney Cemetery.

to a unique Spanish pistol (the suspected murder weapon), which was easily traced to Schifflett by an officer, Andy Thibault, who had dealt with him years earlier for a coin theft; Schifflett was arrested on June 22, 1980.

Stepney Road leads us about four miles eastward and away from Union Cemetery and the Easton Baptist Church, bringing us to the doorstep of the Our Lady of the Rosary Chapel at 15 Pepper Street, Monroe, and the adjoining Stepney Cemetery.

Adjacent to the Stepney Green in the village of Stepney, an offshoot of Monroe, the grounds were established in 1794. This graveyard was otherwise known as Beardsley Plain Cemetery or Birdsey's Plain Cemetery. As if it weren't haunted before, having the area's controversial demonologist Ed Warren interred here in August 2006 has undoubtedly aroused a soul or two.

In 1839, the Greek Revival–style Birdsey's Plain Methodist Church was known as one of the "Twin Churches" on the Stepney Green, built by Hanford Hull. The Our Lady of the Rosary Chapel, as it has been known since 1973 when it was sold to the Orthodox Roman Catholic Movement, has been touted as hosting "the most exorcisms in the U.S." and is a church that strictly follows the traditional Latin Mass (Dominican Rite), with services and liturgy spoken completely in Latin. The pastor there is "Bishop" Robert McKenna, well known for his work as an exorcist.

Clearly posted next to the entry doors of the church is a list of strict rules regarding conduct, dress code and seating arrangements. Heaven forbid you don't abide by them during services.

There are innumerable ghost stories attached to this extended plot of land, the most popular being that of the White Lady, a ghostly figure that remains earthbound and, to this day, unidentified. She has been reportedly seen in and around both of the graveyards for over sixty years now. She appears in a diaphanous white nightgown or wedding dress, gliding between the two locations.

More than one version exists of accounts of firemen slamming their pickup trucks into the white-clad spirit during her occasional breakouts from the confines of the iron fences.

Bishop Robert McKenna in contemplation while strolling through the Stepney Cemetery.

The St. Michael statue. It is only befitting that the symbolism outside of the church, depicted in this statue of good overtaking evil, truly represents the battle for possession of souls that takes place inside the church through the rites of exorcism of demonic spirits.

In one such rendition, a fireman by the name of Ronald Veschi was said to have struck her after viewing the road in front of him take on an eerie red glow and seemingly transform into the cobblestone street that once lay there. Instantaneously to his right he saw a man with a short-brimmed cap (other accounts say straw hat) seated beside him in the passenger seat of his truck. He looked back to the road just in time to see the glowing image of a woman in white with hand outstretched, alarmingly close to the front end of his vehicle. Veschi couldn't stop in time. He heard a thud and felt an impact; instantly checking, he found that the truck was visibly dented but that there were no signs of the woman, her blood or her bones.

No one to this day has ever figured out who she really is or was in her physical lifetime. There is, however, a gravestone within Union cemetery, a few rows down to the left of the main gate, inscribed with the name Harriet B. Seeley, who died May 28, 1853, age twenty-seven years and six months. Also etched into the marker was "Wife of Ezra S. Seeley," and underneath that was a notation that their infant son died on May 21, 1853. This coincides with tales of the White Lady wherein she has been seen and videotaped as a

Left: Headstone to Harriet Seeley's grave—the only stone in the row that is knocked over. Some folks speculate that the identity of the infamous "White Lady" may be Harriet.

Below: The Easton Sinkhole. Situated behind the Easton Baptist Church, this has been a watery grave for at least two men. A blue mist appeared on the film as I photographed the area this past June 2009.

translucent woman in white who appears as an ethereal being, transparent yet still effectively tangible. In these sightings of her, she seems to be looking down and around the ground for something. Harriet Seeley might fit the description of one of the suspects in our efforts to uncover the mysterious identity of Easton's infamous "Lady in White." For reasons unknown, her particular gravestone has been toppled over. Righting it might be one of Harriet's missions on the earthly plane, or possibly the young yet deceased mother is on an otherworldly quest—searching in vain, grieving the loss of her long dead son; however, that's all speculation.

Another possible identity of the White Lady is that of Ellen Smathers, wife of John Smathers, the man whose body was found in a sinkhole behind the church, weighted down with iron chunks in his pockets; Richard Dean Jason later confessed to the murder. The family who bought the Smathers' property in the 1970s had contacted Cosmic Society in the 1990s by sending newspaper articles and other "documented" facts of restless spirits of the Smathers clan, not only in Union Cemetery but also in their newly acquired domain.

Another eerie tale was brought to my attention. Mr. George Nott, murdered by his adulterous wife's lover, Elwood Wade, also met with a watery burial before resurfacing to a cold and dark end. But resurface he did, despite the odds and the fact that the trunk had been burdened with lead along with his body. His defiant corpse was found, however, not long after it had been dumped to descend to the depths of the murky swamp in the wooded area behind the graveyard's church known as the sinkhole. I received the letter below from one of Wade's descendants:

Dear Miss Kent,

I'm looking for pictures or information on Elwood B. Wade, and ran across your website. I have some information about the Wade case. He was my great-grandfather. He was married with two young children, but involved with Ethel Hutchinson Nott, who was married to a man named George Nott. Elwood Wade came over one Sunday morning in 1920 shortly after a loud fight between the married couple and murdered Mr. Nott. He then put Mr. Nott's body in a trunk and threw it in the swamp near Easton. There are accounts during the trial where he kissed Mrs. Nott several times, even in front of his own wife, my great-grandmother. Mrs. Nott was not killed. She was sentenced to life in prison, and after that she disappears. Elwood was found guilty of murder and hanged.

I found my information through the New York Times *archives. If I can provide you with any more info, please let me know!*

Jennifer Wicklund

The case was the "O.J." trial of its era, with the September 1, 1920 through June 3, 1921 *New York Times* headlines reading like something straight out of a Hollywood blockbuster movie script:

CONFESSES HE SLEW CT MAN
Elwood Wade Killed Broker Found in Trunk in Easton Swamp, He Admits

ACCUSED VICTIM'S WIFE
She and Two Men Are Held for Murder—Weapons Discovered in Barrel

WIFE IS ACCUSED IN MURDER CASE
Handed Him the Knife Which Killed Her Husband, Says Bridgeport Man

CHILD'S STORY OF MURDER
Victim's Daughter Testifies Wade Stabbed Nott as He Fell on His Own Porch

MRS. NOTT SHRINKS FROM MURDER KNIFE
Identifies Weapon Which Wade Says She Gave Him to Slay Her Husband

COLLAPSES WHILE IN COURT
She and the Confessed Killer and Johnson are Held on First Degree Charge

BAR CROWD AT NOTT TRIAL
Widow and Two Accused Men are Held for Grand Jury

HOLDS WADE ALONE GUILTY
Connecticut Prosecutor Says State Will Prove He Murdered Nott

WADE KISSES WIDOW—STARTS RIOT IN COURT
Accused Man's Caress before His Own Wife Is Followed by Blow by Deputy

CROWD MOVES TO SEIZE HIM
He is Rushed Out of the Room, while Both Women Faint, Mrs. Nott for the Second Time

MRS. NOTT DESCRIBES HUSBAND'S MURDER
Lays Whole Blame on Wade, Saying He Repeatedly Struck Victim with Iron Bar

DEFENSE TO OPEN TODAY
Wade's Plea Will Be Insanity, but He Also Claims That Mrs. Nott Did the Killing

WADE'S RELATIVES PLEAD HE IS INSANE
Father, Mother and Wife Whom He Spurned Declare Accused Murderer Is Irresponsible
COULDN'T LEARN AS A CHILD
Former School Teacher Says He is Backward—Grandfather Died in an Asylum

WADE IS INSANE ALIENISTS DECLARE
Dr. Diefendorf of Thaw Trial Fame Finds Accused Murderer Mentally a Child

ADMISSION BY THE STATE
Witness for Prosecution Says Prisoner Is Undeveloped
Wife Ignores Wade's Smile

WILL SAY MRS. NOTT DROVE WADE TO KILL
Counsel for the Defense Will Seek to Show That Wife Caused Husband's Murder

PRISONER CALLED SANE
His Wife Becomes Hysterical and Is Carried From Court Room—Testimony Completed

WADE CONVICTED OF FIRST-DEGREE MURDER; SLAYER OF NOTT TAKES HIS FATE CALMLY

WADE THANKS JUDGE FOR DEATH SENTENCE
Murderer of Nott Jests about Hanging as He Leaves the Courtroom

NOTICE OF APPEAL FILED
Execution Stayed Pending Decision—Mrs. Nott and Johnson to Be Tried
Next Month

MRS. NOTT RECEIVES LIFE IMPRISONMENT
New Documentary Evidence Causes Her to Plead Guilty to Second Degree
Murder

CARRIED FROM COURTROOM
Goes Immediately to Wethersfield to Begin Her Sentence—One Year for
John Johnston

In the end, Elwood Wade joked about being able to "taste the cider already," a twisted pun on what a noose would do to his Adam's apple. Mrs. Nott was released from the Connecticut State Farm and Prison for Women (Niantic Correctional Institution) in Niantic, Connecticut, on May 4, 1937. She lived for another forty years with her son, George Jr., in New Jersey. "Junior" enlisted in the navy during World War II, and afterward he and his mother lived in Massachusetts and New Hampshire until their deaths— Ethel in 1978 and her son in 1992. It was said that George never married and dedicated his life to taking care of his murderous mom until the last of her days on earth. Or were they her last? Maybe it is her soul so weighted down with guilt over her murdered husband that keeps her anchored to walk the land where he would only float?

Union Cemetery contains graves and fieldstones dating as far back as the 1600s and continues to yield up dirt and space to include present-day burials. It is a bit daunting to walk through the rust-stricken iron gates and immediately be assaulted from the second tombstone in on the left by the name etched on granite: K-E-N-T, no relation that I know of, but especially in a place like this it's a bit unnerving to see my own name engraved on a tombstone.

There are also tales of a ghostly "hobo," a caretaker's spirit who became obsessed with the ghost of a two-hundred-year-dead trapper's spirit that he saw in the vicinity of the cemetery's hills, and the caretaker now glides the length of the wrought-iron fence. Stories of uniformed men who leave no tracks in the snow and actually talk with the witnesses, reports of men dressed very out of season, let alone century, who reply "straight through" when asked where they're going—and then point toward a path that would lead straight through the man-made reservoir! At Cosmic we've been informed of discarnate voices, growling noises, sounds of babies crying, footsteps,

Entrance to Union Cemetery, New England's most haunted graveyard.

"Ghost mist" from the 3:00 a.m. 1996 shoot. This photo has won awards, and most viewers claim to see a skull resembling a woman with long hair and postulate that this could be an image of the "White Lady."

glowing red eyes that seem to follow, stones and rocks being thrown by unseen hands, shadow ghosts and more.

In addition to stories and reports of murder and tragedy around Union Cemetery and the area of the church, cases of occult activities and rituals, vandalism and general destructive behavior, the graveyard is strictly off-limits after dusk—the Easton police force does enforce this, and hundreds of would-be ghost hunters have received tickets of at least seventy-seven dollars in fines and/or been arrested.

I happened to be at Union cemetery one summer night in 1995, taking photos with friends and strangers who had also come for the same opportunity, when an Easton police patrol car pulled up. Whew! I thought "Thank God we're outside the fence." The officer felt sure that there was someone hiding inside the gates and questioned us all as to where "he" was. We all replied that we hadn't seen anyone inside the perimeter while we had been there. He proceeded in down the center road between two iron pillars, one bearing the remnants of a wreath from too many Christmases past. The next thing we heard was "Hey! Hey! Stop it!" The police officer shined his flashlight all over the bent tombstones and gnarly trees, creating a freaky sort of half-assed light show for the rest of us standing by watching, many paces away. He emerged jogging, drained of color in his face and visibly upset. He, too, didn't find anyone inside of the graveyard, but all the while he was searching, he said, "stones and pebbles landed at my feet" as if tossed from some provoking juvenile hiding nearby. He promptly got in his car and left us all with a "Good luck" and a wave to resume our picture taking.

I receive many letters from people who think they may have encountered the White Lady, at times witnessed out of her "normal" confines of Union and Stepney Graveyards. Whether it be the same lady I don't know, but some of these sighting, and others I've been told, suggest that perhaps she is venturing further, reaching out, conceivably frustrated with her situation remaining unresolved for all these many years:

Hi Donna,

I hope this isn't too long winded or rambling, but I like to tell the story from the very beginning.

This happened in the late summer of 1988. Two friends and I were driving around town at about 2:00 in the morning. I was driving, and we had a very bright hand-held spotlight, the kind which plugs into the cigarette lighter. We were on a road which runs behind the Hi-Ho Motel off the Merritt over into Easton. I know the area well. We were near the Smith Richardson Golf Course heading up a hill when a deer ran through my headlights a few hundred yards up the road. I shut them off and drove up to where the deer had run. I had the car stopped, rolled down my window, and intended to shine the light on the deer. Since the light is so bright, I made sure I was holding it completely outside the car and pointed away from us before I turned it on. The night was overcast and very dark, and I couldn't see anything. I held up the light, pointed it into the field and turned it on. Standing exactly where I had pointed it was a woman dressed all in white. She was probably not more than fifty feet from us, standing in grass up to her knees. She looked to be older, maybe in her sixties. Her hair looked long and was down over her back. She was wearing a long nightgown, with sleeves and cuffs which came down over her hands. The reflection of the light off of her was so bright we could barely look at her.

She stood there completely motionless, staring directly at us and into a light ten times brighter than the headlights on a car. I held the light on her for three or four seconds, shut it off, turned the headlights back on and got out of there. At the first stop sign, I turned to my friends, and we all agreed on what we'd seen. We were all visibly shaking. I went back the next day to try and find an explanation as to why an old woman would be out there at that hour, but the area is just a field with no houses anywhere.

I went back to school that fall, and shortly thereafter stories started to appear in the town newspaper about people seeing a similar person a few miles north near the town of Easton. The descriptions of what others had seen were very close to what we witnessed. I assume she's the same person, even though we saw her quite a distance from where the majority of her activity was reported.

Hope you find our contact interesting. Nothing much happened, but if you had been in the car with her staring back at you, you may think differently.

—*Dave Shannon*

Here's another:

Dear Donna and Cosmic Society,

I happened upon your website while doing some family history research and found it very interesting. I don't know if you still receive mail regarding the site or the pictures within, but I agree that these cemeteries are spooky. Several generations of my father's family are buried in Stepney Cemetery.

When I was a kid, my father would bring my sisters and I to the cemetery around Memorial Day each year to clear weeds and tall grass and plant geraniums around the family headstones. Though I never saw anything unusual (these visits were always early in the day), I would get very upset when asked to bring the grass clippings and weeds to the compost pile at the back of the cemetery. I don't know why, but I was absolutely terrified to go back there, even in broad daylight. On your site I see the stories of the sink hole behind Union cemetery, and the bodies found within that supposedly haunt, but are there any stories regarding Stepney?

My father passed away in 1995 and is now buried there with his parents and grandparents. In keeping with our family tradition, my sisters and I visit several times a year to clean around the family headstones and plant flowers. I no longer feel the unexplained fear that I once felt, so maybe it was just my childhood imagination, but maybe you know of others who have had similar experiences.

Thanks for posting the stories and photos regarding these cemeteries and please remind your reader that while researching and photographing unexplained phenomena is fine, cemeteries are not amusement parks, and the stones and monuments found in them may represent lost loved ones of still grieving families.

Sincerely,
Patty Northrop

And another:

To: Donna Kent
From: Jamie Hearns
Subject: Union Cemetery

Several friends and I recently took a trip to Union Cemetery and had quite an experience. A friend of mine took 3 pictures in the cemetery, depicting what seem to be several thousand orbs in each picture. The friend taking the pictures found scratches on her arm later that night, although she had been wearing long sleeves. Another friend found scratches on her leg after we left the cemetery, in the same place her keys had been laying and then lifted and been floating in the air before that. Also, in the cemetery, we all felt a presence and decided to leave. We were unable to jump over a fence that I easily could have just stepped over. We each tried one by one and were unable to touch it. When we reached the gate, I let my friends run to the car and I took a few steps back into the cemetery and held my cross up in front of me. We heard footsteps chasing us before that, but when I raised the cross they stopped and the presence seemed to dissipate. I ran back to catch up to my friends. When we left in the car, the driver and front passenger both heard strange noises but no one else did. These were also the two girls who were scratched. We pulled over and I held the hands of both girls separately while holding my cross, and they claim the noises ceased. I continued doing this with them and other friends throughout the night when they reported strange feelings, and by the time we reached our destination—our friend's house—the right arm of Jesus, on my crucifix, had almost broken off entirely somehow; as if something had hit it and pushed it inward. Then, when I helped someone a final time, or whatever it was I was doing, the arm fell to the floor. We have 3 pictures depicting orbs in the cemetery and faces on a headstone.

Sincerely,
Jamie, Rick, Tricia, Joe, and Janine

My reply:

Dear Jamie,

Thanks for sharing your story with us at CosmicSociety.com. Some questions arose while reading your letter:
1. I wondered if any or all of you had included some sort of pre–picture taking prayers of protection or any type of ritual of that nature?
2. Concerning the two sets of scratches: What type of scratches were they? How many, how deep, were they bleeding, etc? How long did it take before they went away?
3. Tell me in more detail of the keys floating…who witnessed it and what actually happened? How heavy the key ring was and how far up/over/ wherever did they float? Did they float up and then right to left or vice versa? What area of the cemetery did this happen in?
4. When you sensed the presence and decided to leave—tell me more about that. Was anyone trying to make spiritual contact in any way other than through photography? (Some people don't realize that this is a direct form

of spirit communication even though we may not fully or even partially understand the dynamics of why or how spirit energies end up on our film and in photos.) Was anyone asking questions out loud to any spirits? Were you afraid of the presence? Why? What if anything did it convey to you or the others?

5. The fence incident—Did it feel as if you and your friends were "blocked" from getting over it? Did it seem as if there was some sort of force field or something preventing you from getting over the fence? I need more detail on exactly how it felt for each of you.

6. What type of "strange noises" did your friends hear that the others did not? Was it talking, whispering, knocking, etc.?

7. What are the ages of everyone involved? What, if any or none are the religions or belief systems of those who were involved? (I realize you, Jamie are Christian from what you've told about holding and using the cross to help drive back the presence you felt.)

8. Why or for what purpose did you guys go to the cemetery in the first place? (Intention and motivation are extremely important aspects in these types of pursuits and are easily recognized by spirits who see us through our auras.)

9. Is or has anyone in the group ever used a Ouija Board or similar spirit communication device? (That's a separate questionnaire in itself!) Is anyone practicing any type of magick? If so, what type and for what purposes?

10. Is anyone experiencing any para-phenomenon now or since the visit to the cemetery? If so, who and what?

I think that's enough questions for you all to answer at this time before we can proceed, though I did want to make a comment on the crucifix and the arm being broken off.

In my opinion, you should not try to fix the arm, rather the piece that broke and fell should be left where it was as it is believed that when one of our objects representing our faith or belief system, representing our source of spiritual protection, has broken (almost always unexplainably) that it was the force behind that object that has just used its power doing just that—protecting us from something harmful and it has served its purpose. If the entire thing is broken it is advised to just leave the object where it landed and get a new one. (This is out of respect to the source of protection and to leave any negative energy that may now be attached to it.)

Thank you again for writing us ~ I hope to hear from you and your friends again soon.

Jamie answered:

Re: Union Cemetery

Hey Donna, sorry to take so long to respond but I've spoken with the others and attempted to answer your questions to the best of our ability:
1. I asked everyone if they felt comfortable asking God for protection and they all said they were. Before we got to the cemetery, we all (as far as I know) asked for God's protection, and again before we reached the cemetery and went in, and once more on the way home. I also didn't want anyone to be taking pictures, because I do things like this to try and contact, and help if I can, spirits that are stuck or choose to stay Earthbound.
2. Tricia's scratches ran down the forearm she was holding the camera with, and they appeared to be done with something sharp and there were three scratches, red but not bleeding. I considered the possibility that she made the marks herself (though I wouldn't know why someone would do this, except maybe for attention) but she noticed the marks as we were leaving the cemetery and I saw her arms uncovered before we got there, and I was following last, next to her. I had my eyes on her the entire time and she couldn't have done something without me knowing. More scratches also appeared on her the night after, though I'm not sure where.
Janine's scratches were on her upper thigh, which she noticed when we got home and she went to use the bathroom. There were ten of them, and when I lined my fingers up with them, the lines fit almost perfect to the spacing of my fingernails. These scratches did not bleed either, however the skin was ripped out of the way, not cut. The scratches appeared where her keys had been floating earlier, as if someone was grabbing for the keys and scratched her in the process.
3. The keys themselves were in Janine's pocket, but the long strap was hanging out. It rose straight out in front of her and she reached for it and pulled it back down and she said there was a good deal of resistance. I didn't personally witness the key strap floating, but I did see her pulling something. I asked her what was wrong and she told me about the strap and I held her hand and she said the force on the keys left. This happened in the back corner of the cemetery, near the church.
4. When we decided to leave, Trish thought she saw a red spot in a picture and she believes red orbs or mists are evil and she said we need to leave. However, at this same time, Joe, Rick, and myself all saw a black shape where she had taken the picture. I saw a large black cloud, approx. eight

by eight feet in diameter, about four feet tall moving slowly towards us and felt that it was very bad, and my stomach dropped when I saw it, though not in fear. When I go near a place that is so-called "haunted" with a bad presence my stomach feels this way. Joe saw a person crouching and Rick saw a shape like I did. I had been talking in my head to the spirits in the cemetery, telling them we weren't there to intrude or disrupt them and I asked them to forgive any footfalls that landed on a grave. I had been holding my free hand (my cross was in the other) open, and felt another hand grasp it gently several times when no one was around me (no one still in their physical body, I guess I should say) and when we were crouching to avoid the headlights of cars we all felt as if there were many more people crouching around us, though it wasn't a bad feeling. Then that particular presence seemed to come out of nowhere and it was all I felt, and it was a very nasty feeling.

5. We all agreed that something was most definitely blocking the fence. We all reached for the fence but we were all unable to touch it. It felt as if something wanted us to stay, but we just wanted out. Rick and I are well over six feet tall and could have merely stepped over the fence. However, this particular fence was blocking all of us from leaving.

6. On the way home from the cemetery, Janine, the driver, jumped and screamed several times, and said she heard a noise like deep breathing and then like several close together impacts underwater, like a slow rumble. Tricia also began to hear this, and Janine stopped in a parking lot. She and I got out and I held her hand and my cross and asked God to send down angels to take away whatever force was in Janine, and if it was another person that had attached to her, to bring him home to God. As soon as we were out of the car she stopped hearing the noise, and after I held her hand, she didn't hear it again that night or after.

7. I, Jamie, am sixteen and though I have no specified sect, I believe in God and Christ. Joe and Rick are both sixteen. Joe was not religious for a very long time, but when I began to get religious again I recommended he do the same and he says when he asks for help from God, the help is there almost instantly. Rick hasn't been a believer for many years, but on the way home from Union he borrowed my cross to say a few prayers. Janine is eighteen, and went to Catholic schools for high school and is currently enrolled in one for college, though she doesn't practice religion really. Tricia is seventeen, soon to be eighteen, and isn't very religious. I'd also like to mention that I had my cross, Joe had a cross on a chain, and Rick was wearing a shirt for the metal band Lamb of God that depicts

Jesus on the front, and none of us were injured. The girls however, wore no crosses or anything.

8. Tricia wanted to go to the cemetery to take pictures. I suppose Janine was interested by it and so were Joe and Rick. I wanted to go there because of the feeling we got on our first visit there when we didn't enter the cemetery. I go to places like Union to try and help or at least comfort earthbound souls, and I could feel that there were many souls stuck at Union.

9. All of us have been discouraged by our parents since we were young against using Ouija boards or anything like that, not because of religious reasons, but because of what Ouija boards can summon.

10. The night after we went to Union, more scratches appeared on Tricia's body, but there was nothing after that for any of us.

Thanks again,
Jamie, Joe, Rick, Janine, Trish

And another:

Hi Cosmic Society,

My name is Kyle. I and my friends are constantly exploring the areas of the paranormal. We have visited Union Cemetery one time, but did not step in the grounds of the cemetery to avoid breaking the law of trespassing. What we encountered there was far beyond what we've ever encountered anywhere before. I have a 97 Ford Escort Station Wagon. There were 5 of us that took the drive from Waterbury to Easton, CT. When we got there, we had a picture that indicated an apparition of a woman in white. Moments after viewing the picture from the digital camera while parked in front of the cemetery, the back hatch of my station wagon opened. Now no one was outside of the car, and there is no way to open it from the inside, except the pull the handle from outside. It scared us! So we pulled out about 30 yards still in clear view of the cemetery where we investigated how it opened, and before closing it, we heard a scream from within the cemetery, yelling for us to "Get Out!" There was no one in the cemetery and no one around but us…

We would love to actually explore the grounds there, and we were wondering how you and your crew were able to gain permission to do it. We tried contacting the City of Easton and the Easton Police but we were unable to gain permission to explore at night. We were wondering if you can help us. C'mon Donna, use your "pull" we would really like to find out how to explore the grounds at night and of course, with permission. Thanks in advance,

–Kyle

The stories and letters continue:

Hello Donna,

I went to union cemetery about 11 years ago with a bunch of my high school friends who wanted to go. Not saying anything to my friends, I went along, but knowing that I am very open and sensitive to ghosts etc….I was not keen on seeking them out.

Everyone went into the cemetery; except me. I was the only one that refused to go in. I had a horrible feeling and frankly, I just don't mess with spirits, so I stood outside the gates. Looking in, I saw many red flashing lights; sort of like lightning bugs in the distance, but bigger and very red, all zipping and flying around like bugs. That was all. I got in my car when we all decided to leave, and my car was dead. The transmission just died then and there.

–Anonymous

And another:

Hey Donna!

I moved to Connecticut from Massachusetts in 2001; it wasn't long before I heard about Union Graveyard and the tales of the White Lady. She is believed to roam the area looking or waiting for someone.

One evening, my husband A.J. and I happened to be driving by it, so I asked him to stop. He hesitated and told me the cops always drive by. Seeing no headlights in the distance anywhere (and it's a dark road!) he reluctantly decided to pull over for a quick minute. No sooner did I get my feet on the ground, when low and behold, here come the blues! Lucky for me I got a few moments to at least glance and get a feel for the area while the officer spent about 5 minutes questioning A.J. and telling him the stories of the graveyard are all bullshit. According to the officer he had, on several occasions, sat by the graveyard all night waiting to get a glimpse of something, anything, but nothing ever happened. Finally we were told to be on our way. Needless to say my husband gave me the old "I told you so!" routine and I got back into the truck.

The next thing I knew, I was hearing audibly the voice of woman (her name was Harriet or Helena, I don't recall) who was angry at the officer for lying about the graveyard and the fact that he had claimed to never see anything. My bottle of soda (which was sitting between my feet on the floor) slammed against the inside passenger door, and the woman was gone. I told A.J. what had just occurred as he wondered how the soda had just done that by itself!

When we got home, I went upstairs and showered. As I was drying off, much to my surprise, there was a large "H" scratched on the front of my torso!!! I yelled for A.J., showed him the marks and he was as shocked as I was! It didn't hurt and it didn't stay for too long. While I should have been scared, I believe I was more excited about the fact that (for me) it confirmed I had gotten the name right, or one of them anyways.

I went back to Union one afternoon and found a headstone of a woman named Harriet, who was smack dab in the middle of some other family; she was married and apparently lost an infant child. Where was her husband? Her child's grave? And why was she in the middle of a strange family? Could she be the White Lady?

—Leanne Root

Here's one from afar:

Hello Donna!

Greetings from Japan! My name is Michael, and I am from Wallingford, CT. Right now I am overseas in Japan serving with the US Navy. First of all I wanted to say that I LOVE your site! Definitely the best site I have seen concerning Connecticut's creepy places. Well, I wanted to add a little experience that I had while making a visit to Union Cemetery a few years ago when I came home on leave.

Two friends of mine and me took a trip to the cemetery one night (I believe it was in early September). We did know about the trespassing laws at night, but our curiosity outweighed the risk of being caught. While we never truly ventured deep into the cemetery, I set up my video camera outside the fence looking in.

After some time of picture taking, and nothing spectacular happening, we decided to pack up and call it a night. We were standing on Stepney

Road and my car was parked on Sport Hill Road. That was also where my video camera was set up. My friends decided to walk back through the cemetery to get to my car so they could take a few more pictures. I, on the other hand, elected to walk towards the church so I could take some photos of my own. After I was finished with the photos, I began to walk down church road to reach Sport Hill Road (I did not, at the time, think that the road would be so creepy). As I walked down the path, I really had a sensation that I should be moving faster. I always listen to my instinct!

Now here is the point…You know when a person walks through dead leaves the crunching sound it makes? Well as I came to the junction of Sport Hill Road and Church Road, I paused to make sure I was in the correct spot. When I paused, I heard the leaves continuing to crunch behind me, as if someone was following me. This was clear as day, I was not imagining it and it was not the wind blowing the leaves around! Well, against my better judgment I turned around, hoping that it was one of my friends following me trying to scare me, or at least a raccoon! I turned around and the noise stopped…and there was nothing there. Needless to say I have never run so fast in my life! I sprinted toward my car barely grabbing my camera on the way. My friends were sitting on my trunk and saw me zooming up to the car yelling to get in!!

Ever since that event, I have always been "creeped out" when thinking of it, BUT, I always thought it was a figment of my imagination. Then I stumbled upon your website yesterday. After reading your investigation of Union cemetery and then your opinion of Church road…My goose bump factor went WELL over 100!! I recalled the event, and now I am very convinced that there was something following me. I thought that you would enjoy some testimony of your work!!

Keep it up!

–Michael

I recently interviewed a woman whose son, a college student, along with some friends spent a night inside the cemetery armed with only a tape recorder and a flashlight. Nothing much happened until about 4:00 a.m., when suddenly two of the four youths saw a bright light start floating toward them. Alarmed that the other two couldn't see what they were witnessing, they shined their flashlight on the ball of light only to watch the flashlight sputter and fail to work. The light proceeded toward them but in doing so began to take the shape of a woman. The two who could see this apparition were becoming hysterical, and all four boys gathered up their things and headed for the car—fast!

It was a week later, back at school that they remembered about the audio tape, inadvertently still inside the recorder. The four gathered around to listen to what they thought would be a replay of their own conversations from that evening inside the graveyard, and assuming correctly, the first twenty minutes were just that.

However…just as they had settled down and concentrated on trying to pick up EVPs, being mindful to refrain from talking, there came a strange, deep male voice, spewing obscenities, threats, cursing and really lewd phrases seemingly directly into the microphone. The clarity was astounding and upon researching a random name heard on the tape, the boy's mother found an obituary column dedicated to the "person" whose voice seemed to emanate from their recorder. It seemed he had been killed by a drunk driver while walking along Black Rock Turnpike in Fairfield, Connecticut, a number of years back. No one could make any sense of this spirit having a connection with Union Cemetery, as the article named a different burial ground for the man. It was then that one of the boys remembered that he had been housesitting at a residence on Black Rock Turnpike, the night they had spent in the cemetery.

We all speculated whether this soul is aimlessly meandering around the area of his death, including the many homes on the street. Why had he communicated with the tape recorder at Union Cemetery? Had the boys been followed there? Did the spirit have foreknowledge of the boys' intentions? From what was said he is obviously a tormented, ragingly pissed-off spirit. Perhaps, he's attracted by like spirits said to haunt Union Cemetery, which has well beyond its share of eyewitness accounts, firsthand experiences and multitudinous photographs that have proven and documented beyond a shadow of a doubt the supernatural and preternatural activity occurring at the churchyard and its surrounding locations.

The fact that the Our Lady of the Rosary Church deals with exorcisms regularly makes for an obvious target for demonic spirits with agendas of their own. Because these types of low-vibration entities often usurp and thrive on the negative energy of others, grieving ghosts or heartbroken earthbound spirits can be victimized beyond the grave, continuing the cycle and perpetuating the "ghost syndrome."

Part of the problem in cleansing these areas, specifically cemeteries, of their spiritual saturation lies in the fact that the majority of the entities hovering around these places are *not* earthbound souls! These are the spirits of negatively inclined entities, many not of human origin. These spirits are not the occasional ghost or those of the dearly departed buried within, but rather entities that thrive on the misery, grieving, loss and sadness of the living people who go to mourn there. Throw in what a cemetery actually represents, death and decay, plus an area that has an obvious "aura of disaster," and all the tragedies, accidents and fatal consequences that have befallen this region along with occultist conjuring, sorcery, black magick and other practices, and this once consecrated ground now seems anything but.

Certainly there are lost and confused souls who have not crossed over properly, the "White Lady" being one of them, but as I have felt all along, there is a lot more going on here than "ghosts."

THE CURTIS HOUSE, INCLUDING ST. PAUL'S EPISCOPAL CHURCH AND CEMETERY

Originally, the Orenaug Inn structure was built in Woodbury, Connecticut, in 1734 by the Reverend Anthony Stoddard for his grandson of the same name. The doors opened as the Curtis Inn in 1754, and the premises were operated by the younger Curtis. Passing through the hands of over thirty owners, the inn was named for four unrelated Curtis (some spelled "Curtiss") families in town who had, at different times, lived in the house. Two hundred years later, the Hardisty/Brennan family bought the Curtis House, and it has remained in the family since 1954 and to this day is operated by the Brennans. It is claimed to be the oldest continuously operated public house in the state of Connecticut.

The building has gone through many structural renovations and additions over the years. The entire second floor was originally a ballroom that was later converted into additional guest rooms due to popular demand.

In 1900, the roof was raised and a third floor laid out to accommodate eight guest rooms, which then owner Levi Curtis was anxious to fill after spending a cost of $400 for the entire project. Levi anticipated a major boom in the newly scheduled trolley service. Mr. Curtis earned the claim to "Every Modern Comfort, Every Ancient Charm" by shrewdly maintaining the home's historic charm, as well as adding modern aspects to the house.

The lower-level "Pub Room" was built in the 1950s, during which time a ghostly man was disruptive to workmen during the renovations. The owners felt that "he" might not have wanted any changes made to the dwelling.

The Curtis House Inn dressed in the spirit of the holidays. *Courtesy of T.J. Brennan.*

Currently, the main house has a total of sixteen guest rooms, all with four-poster canopied beds, ten of which have private baths. A common bath is shared by the other six rooms and the more thrifty guests. There is a picturesque footbridge connecting the former carriage house to the main grounds. The carriage house holds four more guest rooms.

Present-day dining facilities accommodate about 250 people, including the banquet area. Aside from its historic character, the inn's reputation for exceptional Yankee fare makes it a regular choice of local businesses; the Curtis House hosts seminars, conferences and special holiday festivities. The menu features chowders and bisques, flaky crusted potpies, all types of roasts, ocean-fresh seafood and desserts baked on premises. Haunted Connecticut Tours occasionally adds the Curtis House as a stop on one of our area tours and have always been sincerely welcomed, efficiently served and, needless to say, well fed!

The Curtis House, with its antique locale, is a fitting companion and merely paces away from a few of Connecticut's most haunted locations, teeming with colonial history. Many of the nearby homes date back to the 1600s. The Glebe House is a ten-minute walk away, and St. Paul's Episcopal Church, with its adjoining graveyard, is closer still. Through one of its former owners, the Curtis House is intricately linked to these places.

Lucius Foote owned the inn from 1852 to 1857. One winter's night, there was a large card game at the inn with Mr. Foote being the lucky winner of a very large pot. It was bitterly cold out but for some reason he took leave on foot; cutting through St. Paul's Episcopal Church cemetery seemed like a timesaving idea. No one knows where Lucius was headed, but he didn't get far. Unfortunately, it wasn't a lifesaving idea or route he chose; Lucius Foote was found frozen stiff in the work barn of the church. It took three days to thaw the man out to perform an autopsy, the results of which turned up inconclusive as to the cause of his death. Townsfolk had suspicions of murder when the winning jackpot was never found alongside his body. They gravely considered the afterlife ramifications of the deadly deeds that had been committed on sacred ground.

His spirit is often sensed in room 1 of the Inn. One female guest reported being bumped and pushed over after the ghost seemingly entered the room. Other folks who had stayed in that room would relay similar stories: "The ghost would come in, take off his boots and say, 'He had a bad ride.'" A psychic who once slept in room 1 felt the man in the room and his attempt to crawl into her bed. "I just moved over and let him lay

St. Paul's Episcopal Church, Woodbury, Connecticut. The church itself is a place of divine light; however, the adjoining graveyard holds secrets to a dark and deadly past.

down, too," she said. Other tales of room 1 say that a man enters the room with loud thudding footsteps, like those of someone wearing heavy boots. He then stands next to the bed and proceeds to remove his work boots and drop them to the floor.

There was talk of a strange photo of man who had the garb of the old-time riders taken in the pub area when nobody was in the room, but no one at the inn can remember what became of it. Because of the footsteps often heard, it is believed by the staff that the liquor storage room is where he probably hangs out for privacy.

It's a fact that before King Solomon's Temple was built nearby the local Freemasons held their meetings at the inn. Using a mysteriously separate secret entrance somewhere on the outside of the building, they would gather for their esoteric functions and rituals. In one transfer of title to the building, the Freemason's right to privacy is recorded as "encompassing Masonic business and including protecting the whereabouts of the secret entryway," which happens to still be topic of debate.

Cosmic Society was invited to conduct an investigation of the inn in September 2005, and with such a large facility, we had limited time for our investigation. We set up our equipment in a timely fashion and commenced to concentrating fully on the task at hand.

We had five separate cameras running in different areas of the main house, which is where we focused our lenses and psychic senses. One camera was used to interview the owner and a few of the employees; T.J. Hardisty was most forthcoming and informative, providing us with several stories and anecdotes regarding her life at what she has always called home and those of the dead that did so previously.

She told us about "Joe," a former employee who used to work with T.J. He had a particular way of sitting in certain chairs and would always smoke cigarettes. T.J. has not seen him herself, but at least two of the staff have witnessed his presence and returned white-faced from the basement to tell her about their individual experiences. In the afterlife (just like in his "real" life), Joe likes to sit in the basement and eat potatoes (he would go down there to "hide" and eat). The staff finds the chairs placed exactly how he had them at times. Once a young male employee came back from getting firewood and saw a man, all alone, sitting and eating a plate of potatoes. The employee described Joe perfectly—what he wore and did and where he sat. Joe died twenty years prior to this employee's tenure; he had no way of knowing him or any prior knowledge of the hungry ghost.

Guests hear noises coming from above them in the attic—walking and moving—when staying overnight in room 5. When T.J. mentioned that a group of students had experiences in this room, this confirmed the vibes I had picked up when I entered of feeling watched and definitely not alone.

Room 16 is said to host a doting female apparition; paying special attention to male guests staying in the room, she tucks them into bed, fixes the covers and may even crawl in next to them! (Perhaps she should spend time in room 1.) One woman felt a shove while sleeping and even got bruised by it but laughed it off, saying that it seemed like she "was just in the way" and that the ghost "did not mean to hurt me, but it may not have wanted me there, either."

One female worker felt that the dining room was where a female spirit helps to oversee catering functions, and one day, obviously overwhelmed and perspiring, she told T.J. how she suddenly felt "at peace because this woman was taking care of her, and making sure all was well."

The portrait of Anthony Stoddard is not without its quirks, and the story how it ended up at the inn is even stranger. Peter Stoddard is a modern-day ancestor of Anthony Stoddard. One day, while looking for the Woodbury Town Hall, he saw the inn and stopped for directions. He noticed a plaque above the front door bearing the same name as his own. After some conversation, Peter mentioned that he had acquired a portrait of Anthony Stoddard from Yale and, as promised, sent a reproduction to T.J., which now hangs in the dining room. Initially, after framing, it was hung in the sitting area, across from the reception desk, and many bizarre events transpired. One lifelong employee felt especially upset by it—she felt that the eyes were watching from all angles, and she was never comfortable near the portrait. Since there, it has been a source of discomfort for many employees. So many complaints prompted T.J. to move it to the dining room, now with his own wall, a "shrine" of sorts; the bizarre events seem to have eased up. He may have been upset at what he saw happening from the foyer.

In the foyer are framed photographs of T.J.'s brother-in-law, William I. Brennan, CW3 U.S. Army, awarded with a Bronze Star in Operation Iraqi Freedom, who was recently killed in Iraq. T.J.'s daughter (niece of William) was having trouble coping with her uncle's demise and began having vivid dreams of him. T.J. strongly feels William's spirit at the inn as an overseer and protector of the family. As I stood in front of the wall of pictures and decided to take a few of my own, my camera batteries went completely dead. I took it as a sign that William was acknowledging my presence and

The hallway entrance to room 16 at the Curtis House Inn.

efforts to relate the story of the souls, both living and dead that reside at Connecticut's oldest inn.

There are many reports of things being moved and broken or of putting something down only to turn around and find it vanished. In 1976, the building suffered a roof fire, and one of the more dangerous and "freakish" incidents happened one evening when T.J. was tending the small fire in the foyer's fireplace—her arm and face were burned when the fireplace "blew up" for no apparent reason.

The attic is a hotbed of activity. The crawl space is dense, and I visually saw orbs and photographed them. I discerned the energy of a possible former slave. Whoever it was it seemed subservient and submissive. I felt the person was hiding and scared of being discovered. My hair was tugged more than once while up there. Investigator Brian felt an "electric feeling" and had his hair stand on end in the attic.

Cosmic's video and audio results included evidence from the attic on audio recorder #4: silence, brief static followed by garbled, indistinguishable words and then clearly a man's voice saying "behind the walls." Video cameras #1

The beautifully creepy portrait of Anthony Stoddard. Strange occurrences connected to the portrait caused staff to relocate it to the dining room, easing the activity and the constant feeling of being watched.

and #2 try to refocus a number of times with no visible cause, and orbs were caught on film on camera #1, which was seen on the remote monitor. The tri-field electromagnetic frequency (EMF) meter spiked at eighty in the attic—no one was present; this was viewed and recorded on camera #1.

Photos from my first visit, which was midday, May 2005, include orbs in the attic.

Second-visit photos include a blue orb in the attic, orbs in the dining room and faint orbs in some of the guest rooms. Brand-new camera batteries died out completely in room 18. Batteries in another camera were completely exhausted after taking only three shots in room 5.

We left the inn, with its residents and resident ghosts, satiated; from the number of psychic events and documented stories obtained to all of our evidence caught electronically, we had our hands full with the new task of going over it all and distinguishing natural causes from true paranormal occurrences. I think we all left a few pounds heavier in our waistlines; we ate from the moment we arrived until we left. I think it was the second helping of beef brisket that put me over the edge or maybe the strawberry shortcake that followed. It was worth it, but I'll have to diet before going back again!

THE GLEBE HOUSE MUSEUM AND
GERTRUDE JEKYLL GARDENS

Nestled in the cozy hamlet of Woodbury, Connecticut, is the Glebe House, a place unlike any other museum I've ever investigated. In May 2005, the owner of the Haunted Connecticut touring company, Betty Cordellos, and I went to visit. The sun shone brightly, and we were anxious to begin a walk through the homestead. I struggled with my equipment and camera bags as Betty walked on ahead and introduced herself to Judith Kelz, the educational director at the museum.

I hadn't even reached the front door when the very first words out of Judith's mouth were "This place is *not* haunted!" and I immediately thought of Shakespeare's "The lady doth protest too much, methinks." As always, I chose to rely on my psychic abilities coupled with electronic equipment to determine whether "the Glebe" was haunted before I accepted her words at face value. In fact, it *did* look like a beautiful and tranquil place, and initially I felt drawn to its quaint, colonial beauty.

Yet what at first seemed a remote possibility for a haunting soon proved to be my most intense and dangerous case of 2005. Learning the dark history of the place would soon overshadow the brilliantly sunny atmosphere outside.

The First Book of Woodbury Land Records shows that in 1659 an Indian deed reports that Thomas Wheeler purchased the land parcel of fifteen by ten miles from Pomperaug tribe sachem Tantannimo and four of his sagamores. Records show that all parties concerned felt the deal to be reasonable. Settlement of the land in 1672 resulted from breaks in the beliefs systems of residents of Stratford, Connecticut, and the differences

Left: The Glebe House Museum and Jekyll Gardens.

Below: The Glebe House at dusk.

of religious opinions was "ushered in by thunderings and lightnings and earthquakes ecclesiastical."

I learned about the Glebe House's rich early history: tragic chronicles of violence, political oppression, rebellion and the resulting local legends—legends that many still believe today.

"Glebe" comes from the Latin word *glēba* or clod, meaning a plot of land belonging or yielding profit to an English parish church or an ecclesiastical office and, archaically, the soil or earth; land.

The current Glebe House was built in 1750 in Woodbury, Connecticut, but the original foundation and two rooms date back to the 1650s. The Marshall family, from New York City, moved into the house in 1771 and lived there until 1786. Family members included head-of-household John Rutgers Marshall, the first permanent minister for the local Episcopal church (Church of England); his wife Sarah; and their nine children. They owned two or possibly three slaves who shared space on the second floor. The Reverend Marshall and his family were very well liked and respected in Woodbury, a large community with about five thousand people (at the time, Woodbury encompassed Southbury, Oxford, South Britain, Roxbury and Bethlehem). It was, for them, a simple, peaceful and pious life.

However, serenity for the Marshalls was soon cut tragically short, and conflict would surround the occupants as the colonials' discontent with King George III and his unjust policies increased to the boiling point and soon erupted into armed rebellion.

The American Revolutionary War broke out in 1775, only four years after the Marshalls moved into their home. Woodbury's militia was called to arms. While most other Anglican ministers fled to Nova Scotia and England, John Marshall courageously remained in the Glebe House. In Connecticut, during wartime, only 6 percent of men still claimed loyalty to England. Woodbury's population was especially zealous in its devotion to the cause. It was not a safe haven for anyone officially representing England or its church.

The Reverend John Marshall, England's local representative, was immediately assumed an enemy of the revolution. Politics and hatred erased any warm feelings toward him, and his former friends and neighbors placed Marshall under house arrest that same year. The only allowance they granted was a walk to St. Paul's Church on Sundays to conduct services, right across the street, up through the cemetery and straight back home. The terms of this one-day amnesty each week also accorded Reverend Marshall the privilege of saying anything he chose during his service, even praise for the king and England, without arrest or assault. Every Monday, however, the colonials revoked this paltry reprieve for the rest of the week. Groups of "inspectors" dragged him out of the house almost every day (except Sunday) and beat him ruthlessly for preaching the words "Pray for the King, Church and England." This chain of events repeated every week for some time. Marshall had stated that his first duty was to God and therefore England, and so he continued his defiant prayer, regardless of the consequences, believing it his sacred obligation.

Even though the local rebels and Patriots easily forced their way into the house and captured him in the beginning, the inquests became fruitless later on. Why was John Marshall never home? Unbeknownst to his enemies, Marshall somehow hid successfully from those who entered and searched for him. But how? Statements from his family that John was not present were met with skepticism by the so-called inspectors. Dismissing the family's denials, they doggedly ransacked the house during each "visit" yet still never discovered him. Eventually, they would give up for the day and look elsewhere. Just as the family cleaned up the damage and mess, more inspectors would return and tear the house apart again. It was a cycle of terror and hardship for the Marshall family, yet, incredibly, with his family's undaunted support, he remained in the house undetected. Allegedly, Marshall often chose to disregard his house arrest and was frequently ambushed by attackers, who stoned him upon his leaving the front door or pulled him from his horse, beating him mercilessly.

Unfortunately, the accumulated injuries from these outside beatings took their toll on his body and led to his death at age forty-six.

But the question remained: how did he so effectively hide inside the house?

In 1925, the Glebe House first opened as a historic landmark and museum. During renovations, a long-forgotten panel was removed from the front staircase. It revealed two incredible discoveries. First, immediately visible, was a previously undetected space built halfway into the ground, right below the main staircase. Large enough for a human being and some supplies, it was a perfect and very secret hiding space. It was accessed through a false back built into the dining room hutch. Anyone could push easily and quickly through the false hatchway and disappear almost instantly from the first floor of the house. This almost certainly explains Reverend Marshall's ability to avoid his persecutors. One can surmise that he built it secretly during his ordeal. This hiding place was so ingenious that it took 150 years of searching for anyone to find it! The mystery had finally been solved. But the second 1925 discovery hinted at an even more incredible possibility.

Glebe House Museum docent Robert Dreher poses in period clothing much like former owner John Marshall would have worn.

Right behind and below the hiding place was what appeared to be the entrance to an underground tunnel! Had one of Woodbury's most mysterious and persistent legends been confirmed?

For over 150 years, many theories existed about John Marshall's hiding places. The most exciting was the rumor of a secret underground tunnel system at the Glebe House. This supposition had been passed down from generation to generation, growing to mythical proportions. Yet, with each year that passed, the location of the purported tunnel proved just as elusive to seekers as Reverend Marshall was to his tormentors. Many had tried to find it since the late 1700s. "The Legend of the Tunnels" captured the imaginations of many. But did any tunnels really exist?

The most accepted version is that the underground tunnel(s) spanned from the Glebe Home to the Jebez Bacon home, within view just down the road and in the hollow. Mr. Bacon was known as a fellow Tory (English Loyalist) and was the wealthiest man in Woodbury. One can easily see why this theory emerged: two British Loyalists could plot more easily in unfriendly territory if they could travel and meet undetected. A tunnel would be an ideal means. Others believe that the tunnels lead not only to the underside of the Bacon residence but also to the adjoining church and cemetery (obviously conspiracy theorists have been around forever). Was it through these secret passages in 1783 that ten clergy members crawled in order to carry out their plans of a clandestine assembly to elect Episcopal minister and Loyalist Reverend Samuel Seabury as the first American Episcopal bishop in the new nation? The nomination and its acceptance would imply the separation of church and state and religious open-mindedness in the New World. This historic vote would put the Glebe House on the map as the birthplace of American Episcopalianism.

Alas, people would have to wait another fifty-five years before a real, scientific search and analysis would be finally undertaken.

Responding to intense interest in the passageway fable, the director of the Glebe House Museum in 1980 set out to investigate the secret tunnel legend. In order to accomplish this most effectively, the director invited archaeologists and geologists from Yale University to help with that task. For six or seven summers, they came and they dug. They uprooted the entire yard doing scientific studies and tests. Their conclusions were disappointing to many, but others still hold hope regardless of the evidence.

The Yale study determined that a tunnel or tunnels could not possibly exist in the area for these reasons: one, these dwellings are in the hollow, which means lower elevation drainage areas. Water seeks the lowest level. The water table was too high in the 1770s for the earthen walls to contain a tunnel for any substantial period of time, and that is still true today. Also, the nearby river increased the water levels even more. Secondly, the townsfolk themselves couldn't possibly keep such a thing a secret!

Interestingly, this contradicts documented stories by the historical society of independent interviews with people regarding their experiences together and alone—spent inside the tunnels. Some of these accounts date back to the early 1920s.

As I began equipment setup to interview Judith, I learned that the only room in the building with an electrical outlet was the office located on the first floor, and with my two battery packs now unexplainably drained (they were fully charged in preparation of the day), this severely limited my videotaping range.

Relying now on only a digital camera for photo documentation, I was impressed with the amount of spirit energy I was picking up and disappointed about the recorder being stationary. One remarkable area is the front room to the left of the front door. It was used as a waking/funeral room where Mr. Marshall performed most, if not all, of the funeral services required of him as clergy. The door leading to the outside of the house from this room was called the "Coffin Door" because it was through there that coffins were carried most of the time.

On the second floor were the former family's bedrooms. The third floor is extremely hot in summer and held small quarters for the slaves. Above that is an attic.

My digital Nikon camera captured a few random orbs (in the areas of the front-room fireplace, the slave quarter's bed, the "Coffin Door" and the dining room closet/hiding spot) while the curator and I moved throughout the homestead and she related tales from the dwelling's checkered past. Psychically, I felt the presence of an angry black person whom I thought to be a female, but I didn't get any sense of her age.

Thinking I'd like to have the Cosmic Society in for a closer look, I arranged for a few members and myself to visit for a nighttime investigation. The case commenced on May 17, 2005, from 8:15 p.m. to 10:00 pm. It was a weeknight, and the group, as well as the docent, had time constraints, rendering our visit to only a few hours in duration.

We followed our usual equipment setup routine, which included video cameras and multiple audio recorders, and then traversed the building taking hundreds of photographs. Nothing seemed to be happening outwardly, but upon later inspection of the photos, many multicolored, opaque and translucent orbs appeared. We finished up and departed on schedule.

After stopping for a bite to eat at a diner closer to home, a former boyfriend Brian and I got in our separate cars to drive to my apartment. As I rounded a corner, my red mustang seemed to speed up on its own and began to spin wildly out of control! It hit a curb and slammed the left front fender into a tree—ruining my rim and popping my tire. A bit shaken, we left the car on the curbside to retrieve and repair the following day.

The next day, as Brian left to retrieve the vehicle, I figured I'd shower and get ready for the day ahead. With both arms up, hands in my hair, shampooing, I suddenly felt a stinging sensation on my right arm. Looking down, there were three red slashes on it. Having gone through this type of "spirit attack" before, I knew to quickly photograph and document the situation in case the marks disappeared swiftly, as often happens. By the time Brian returned, the marks were indeed gone, but I still had the photo to show.

These events signaled a possible negative haunting—something did not want us there! As any experienced ghost hunter can tell you, dark, mean and nasty things from the "other side" *can* follow you home in an attempt to hinder or stop you from investigating them. Becoming concerned about others who had been in attendance the night before, I phoned the group and asked if they had been having any unusual activity. One of our members, Chris Nickerl, had just gotten done listening to his audiotapes and said he had gotten numerous EVP: "Help her!"…"Don't worry!"…"Ohhhh!"…"Yes…I know."

On another tape, a Cosmic member commented how steep the back stairway was, saying "Whoa! That looks like instant death," to which the tape recorder captured an otherworldly female voice hissing in response: "Yesssssss!" There were no females in the room at that time.

Then Chris played me one more EVP over the phone that stopped me cold in my tracks. I couldn't believe the words I heard. It was a high-pitched, altered-sounding voice, screaming, "I'll get in the car!"

Chris, the Cosmic member who played this EVP for me, did not know of my car accident, and when I told him, the other end of the line went silent. We were both frozen in amazement. The current EVP theory is that the voices of humans spirits—those that have passed from earth—sound just like a normal living person on tape, minus the ambience of the room. It's as if the voice is directly imprinted on tape. On the other hand, demonic voices tend to sound altered, as if processed through an echo chamber, and the high frequency sounds like it has been weirdly altered from its original pitch. That last voice fit the description of a demonic voice entirely.

Long-term harassment began every time we initiated plans for a Glebe House follow-up investigation, such as making phone contact or even leaving messages on the answering machine regarding dates for investigation; things began to go wrong.

One night I dreamt that I was investigating the Glebe House, and a dark cloudy mass was following me from room to room. Frightened, I tried to find my way out of the house, with the black "thing" just at my heels. Just then, I was awakened (physically) by my dog barking frantically at the front door. I went right back to sleep but was still half awake, and I found myself in a new dream in which I was lying in my bed just as I really was at the time. I saw the same black cloudy mass following me yet again—only this time it was here in my apartment. It came from the back door and circled through the rest of the apartment, finally stopping abruptly at the French doors that lead to my bedroom. Being that I was half awake, I could still hear Brian snoring lightly and rhythmically next to me. In the next instant, three things happened at the *exact* moment that the "thing" stopped at the bedroom doors (which were slightly ajar): I sat up straight in bed looking at the glass French doors; Brian, still asleep, loudly said, "HELLO!" in a snarling voice; and the "thing" stopped suddenly right at the entrance of the French doors.

Wide awake and unable to fall back asleep, I did what I always do; I grabbed my camera and began snapping photos of the area. I was amazed at what I saw after snapping a few shots of Brian, asleep in bed: an intense yellow, orange and red energy trail that emanated from outside the frame of the photo but in each picture ended at Brian's body.

Two nights later, Brian suggested we do a protection ritual around our bed. I sprinkled salt and holy water and recited some standard prayers. The next morning, at 5:30 a.m., our smoke detector above the bed sounded off very loudly. We checked the entire house for any signs of smoke or fire, even going upstairs to the second-floor apartment and waking the landlord. We found no cause for the alarm to sound. It went off again the next day between one and two in the afternoon, again without any apparent basis. It had never happened before then and has not happened since then.

Next, Brian began to have dreams of the Glebe House:

I awoke from a dream that was disturbing—not quite a nightmare—but one that was very unique. When I have dreams, they are usually in vivid color and I can hear, smell, and feel, etc. This dream had a grayish overall pallor, and it was [like] a completely silent film. It was weird to experience it so tangibly, yet have absolutely no sound. I was in the second-floor slave quarters of the house, looking west. My attention (and alarm) was focused on what looked like an old decaying man, Caucasian, standing right in front of me. His mouth was torn open in a perpetual angry scream, the skin wrinkled and dangling off the edge of his face. His gray hair was falling out, giving him a very mangy look. The scream was directed at me, yet I couldn't tell if he was angry at me, or desperately trying to shriek for my help. His eyes were dark—almost like the black holes in an empty skull. His clothes were worn and hanging in tatters off of his body. He looked like someone who'd been dug up from a grave and his clothes like they had been torn in a struggle. It dawned on me after a moment that his scream was anger at me—because he suddenly moved in at me aggressively, trying to attack me. In the dream, I fended him right off and ordered him to "Stay back!" He hesitated and remained in place, even angrier at this "defeat." The far room (past the slave quarters, behind the man) had a window, and light was shining in through it. There were silhouettes of women in old-style ball gowns passing back and forth like they were busy preparing for something. It struck me that they did not bounce from walking, nor could I perceive any foot motion. They simply flowed back and forth smoothly, as if they were riding a fast conveyor belt, but they were not levitating off the floor. The speed with which they moved felt like people in a hurry to finish something they were doing. The man continued to scream at me as I woke up. This dream repeated itself for several nights, almost exactly the same way, and leads me to wonder if it is a message from something at the Glebe House—something that doesn't want us there poking around.

In October 2005, we kicked off Haunted Connecticut's new Waterbury-area tour, which included a stop at the Glebe House. I had my reservations about bringing guests into the historic museum with all the negativity we'd encountered. Of primary concern was the fact that this would be a very large group of third- and fourth-grade Girl Scouts! After learning that there would be at least fifteen adults, and tailoring the information to suit the youngsters, I hesitantly agreed to the inclusion.

The day went wonderfully. How I wish all my tour groups could be adoring, seven-year-old Girl Scouts! Open-minded and innocent, they asked the most inquisitive questions, and their untainted curiosity actually made me have to stop and think how to answer them at times. Our time was spent without incident, until we reached the graveyard.

The Glebe House is located behind St. Paul's Episcopal Church and across the street from its adjoining cemetery. The burial grounds hold the remains of many prominent families, including the Marshalls. The church was founded in 1740, and at the time "the Glebe" served as the parish rectory.

During our research at the Curtis House, we learned that a man named Lucius Foote had been bludgeoned to death for his poker winnings at St. Paul's Episcopal Church cemetery in the mid-1800s. He was not found until three days later, and it is believed that his angry and aggressive spirit does not want those of the living to enter the confines of the cemetery.

During the tour, the Girl Scouts were allowed to walk around the graveyard randomly. At one point, I heard two of the ladies in the group saying, "Get Donna over here! Just get her over here, now!" I asked what was going on and found two very stunned women. One of their cameras had begun taking pictures on its own and then "hummed a tune," as she put it. I heard it, as did others nearby. "This is impossible!" the woman stated, and as I listened, I realized that it was actually a familiar tune to me—it was a little riff that I made up myself and have been singing/humming for about twenty or so years. *Something* was looking for attention and mimicking me. There was absolutely no rational reason for her camera to have any audible sounds coming out of it, especially of that nature.

As dusk fell, it was time to bring the tour to an end, and I encouraged all of my guests to send in any questionable pictures from our day together. It was less than a week later that I received this letter:

Hi Donna,

It's Margie here, from the haunted tour you did for us on Saturday. First, I want to thank both yourself and your boyfriend for the wonderful job that you did. The girls adored you and we all had a super time. Second, I haven't taken a look at all the pictures yet, but check this one out (the last picture we took at the Glebe House). If you look in the window with the bright light and zoom in, as clear as day my girls and I can make out the image (from the ribs up) of an African American woman. Her eyes are closed, head towards the camera with a beautiful smile. You can see a white bustier-type dress, with black straps and her exposed shoulders, and she is wearing some kind of hat. Do you see it, or are we all losing our minds? Anyway, I did want to give you this email address, so that if you had any good pictures, maybe you could forward a few (especially the coffin where you don't see the orb, then you do). We hope to book another tour next fall in a different territory (actually, the girls said I had to, and as you can clearly see, they run the show). Have a wonderful rest of your weekend! Thank you again for all your help.

—Margie

The investigator's notes from our May 17, 2005 visit and the resulting data and strange occurrences that transpired leave me more baffled and with more questions than when we started this case; here are a few impressions of the Cosmic Society members from our investigation:

Chris N.

Psychic impressions: "Felt the presence of 'someone' watching on second floor."

Gauss meter: Hits and spiking on second floor and attic.

Audio: Several EVPs—see below.

Photos: two or three orb shots on first floor.

EVPs on the second floor: "Yes"…"ohhhh"…"Don't worry" ("Don't worry" did not register on computer sound wave).

EVPs in the attic: "Yes I know" and "I'll get in" were recorded on the Olympus recorder while we were leaving. The only thing was that the recorder was already shut off. It turned itself on again for only ten seconds, which was when the EVP was recorded. The recorder was never manually turned on again by any of us. Also, this is the only "voice" that does not sound like any type of human origin—it sounds demonic.

Funeral room: Cassette recorder that was set up in the funeral room recorded absolutely nothing! No EVPs, no noises—natural or otherwise—not even noises of us walking through, taking photos, talking, etc. The tapes were completely blank even though it was working and the power/record light held power the entire time.

Leanne R.

Psychic impressions: I felt drawn toward the outbuildings—they made me feel a little sad and then scared, nervous and jumpy. I had extremely uneasy feelings in the attic and have been feeling anxious since our arrival.

Photos: Camera problems right away, outside of the house, although the camera worked fine at the cemetery and inside the building.

Donna K.

Psychic impressions: "Second floor made me feel nauseous. I had a pressure headache that usually accompanies the presence of strong spirits. I also had a strong sense of vertigo near the back stairway."

Gauss meter: None.

Audio: None.

Video: The fact that the entire building has only one electrical outlet greatly hindered any substantial videotaping. The camera was actually placed atop a lamp and directed into the huge room that once served as the kitchen and dining area. Poor lighting was also detrimental to filming.

Photos: Orbs immediately outside and plenty on first floor. My camera captured many orbs in the cemetery, visible to the naked eye at some times.

After the Marshalls moved, a silversmith by the name of Gideon Botsford lived there with his wife and eight children until the mid-1800s, and in 1892 three Connecticut clergy bought it as a gift for their bishop, John Williams, for a total of $500. By 1920, the house had seen several owners come and go, and the house and property had been severely neglected. Under the direction of William Henry Kent, from the Metropolitan Museum of Art, New York, the old church homestead was rescued by the Seabury Society for the Preservation of the Glebe House, which took care of repairs, in addition to collecting furniture and money to guarantee that the museum would continue to operate. The Glebe House Museum continues to run seasonally and by special appointment to this very day.

One year after opening, the museum commissioned Gertrude Jekyll, the renowned English horticultural designer and writer, to design an "old-fashioned" garden for the site. Why the plans for over six hundred feet of vegetation and blooms never came to fruition is unknown to history, nor why they were quashed altogether, but in the 1970s, they were rediscovered. In 1989, they were part of a project to complete the Gertrude Jekyll Gardens on the land.

Because of the season, I was unable to view the botanicals, but I noticed that throughout the gardens (which encircle the dwelling) are scattered at least twenty full or partial headstones and footstones. Most of the markers were so worn and aged that no writing was visible, but a few had a name or a date still legible here or there. Used as steppingstones, they could be a source of unrest for those souls that claim these grave markers as their own, coupled with the fact that their final resting spots are no longer marked for remembrance.

No one remembers the identities of these gravestones and the others that are scattered throughout the Jekyll Gardens, and the forgotten footstones are haphazardly used as steppingstones by those who may not even realize what they are walking on.

There is much more going on than meets the eye at the Glebe House and its adjoining properties. All are worthy of a trip for many reasons—obviously its historic and religious value (which most likely has a lot to do with the spirits that remain there), its educational contribution and even the thrills and chills that the place provides. If you do visit, just be respectful and careful and be sure to watch your step on that back staircase—"yessssssss" it's a doozy.

THE CAROUSEL GARDENS RESTAURANT

Located in Seymour, Connecticut, the Carousel Gardens Restaurant is considered the area's most haunted Victorian mansion. Formerly the Wooster estate, those who worked in the now closed eatery believe in spirits and things supernatural because of their occasional experiences with the place. Most, if not all, have witnessed at least one event during their term at the elegant mansion.

The town of Seymour was originally named Chusetown by early settlers in honor of Pequot Indian Chief Joseph Mauwehu, nicknamed "Chuce." European settlers and Indians lived together as friends as more and more people traveled "upriver" from Stratford and set up their homes. The area became too populated to support the traditional Indian way of life, as gristmills, paper mills and corn mills encroached on the abundant Naugatuck River, the town's most valuable natural asset. Chuce and his tribe moved to Kent, Connecticut, to a larger Pequot settlement. The town was later named Humphreysville in honor of George Washington's right-hand man, David Humphreys. In 1850, for reasons unknown, the townsfolk wanted to rename the town Richmond but instead opted for Seymour, in reverence of Governor Thomas Hart Seymour.

Designed by New Haven architect William Allen for Mr. Wooster in June 1895, construction of the estate began and was completed in the year 1894. On his property consisting of about thirty-four acres stood the Victorian mansion, the servants' quarters and the carriage house (now long since gone). William Henry Harrison Wooster was born in Waterbury (then

The Carousel Gardens Restaurant, Connecticut's most haunted Victorian mansion.

Prospect), Connecticut, on July 4, 1840. Mr. Wooster married the late Anna L. Putnam of Springfield, Massachusetts, on August 3, 1867. The couple had six children: five daughters, Anna Thompson, Clara Lee, Louise, Mabel and Helena Ruth, and one son, Horace. Mr. Wooster was considered a "captain of industry" and possessed the qualities of virtue, hard work, enterprise, integrity and foresight. He excelled in the areas of finance, organization and the management of men; he served not only the Seymour Manufacturing Company, its associates and employees, but also was freely devoted to the best interest of the community.

Mr. Wooster served our country during the Civil War in the Union cause, helping to form a company of Connecticut volunteers. He was responsible for founding the Seymour Manufacturing Company, the Seymour Trust and the Seymour Water Company until his death on December 17, 1919, at the age of seventy-nine. He was also the vice-president and director of the H.A. Matthews Manufacturing Company, as well as being a member of the board of education and the building committee for Seymour's first high school. He belonged to the Seymour Congregational Church and served as a superintendent of the Sunday school. In his unimaginable spare time, he was an avid outdoorsman.

The death of William Henry Harrison Wooster was mourned as the passing of the first citizen of Seymour and an outstanding figure in Connecticut industrial circles. His wife Anna L. Putnam Wooster was laid to rest on March 2, 1927, at the age of eighty-six. In his will, Mr. Wooster stipulated that the house be used by his wife Anna as a homestead and, in the event of her death, to be used by his three daughters Louise, Mabel and Helena (no mention of the other two sisters) as a personal homestead and then to be passed on to their heirs jointly. The Woosters are buried at the Trinity Cemetery in Seymour, Connecticut.

Ruth Wooster was the last living relative to reside in the estate, keeping the home in the family until about forty years ago. She was laid to rest at the age of ninety-three on May 22, 1972. It is said that she became quite eccentric in her later years, taking to wearing a fur coat in the middle of summer and entertaining her dogs as dinner guests, with places set for them nightly at her dining table.

In direct opposition of Mr. Wooster's last will and testament, the homestead has been used since Ruth's death by many different owners for as many differing purposes: an office space, a ballet studio, a graphic arts studio, a boardinghouse and, until its closing in 2009, the Carousel Gardens Restaurant.

Paul and Debbie Sciaraffa purchased the estate in September 1993 and opened the luxurious restaurant, decorated with real carousel horses, most of which came from an auction of the Danbury Fairgrounds. Paul owns the original blueprints of the mansion, which show the foyer as the former carriage porte where horse-drawn carriages would stop and let off passengers.

The present-day coat room was used as a washroom and once contained a sink. Just beyond this on the right is the main staircase of the home with original oak railing, which has been an area of high paranormal activity. People of all ages have commented or complained of feeling dizzy and almost losing their balance here. A Cosmic Society investigation in the fall of 1997 determined that there was an energy portal in the area of the second landing from the bottom.

The taproom or bar was once used as a library and study area. Behind the taproom, you'll find what was once the parlor, and the original kitchen stove is now housed in this area as a showpiece.

The music room was located just past the taproom and was where Ruth played the piano. Windows were removed to accommodate the area as a restroom, and the servants' stairway is located just to the right of the kitchen doors off the main hallway. The kitchen remains in the same area as it was originally. There is one other room on this floor, and it is decorated with stained-glass windows, used as a dining area and is known as the Garden Room.

On the second floor, to the right of the staircase, is the room used as Horace's bedroom in earlier times. It served as the master bedroom for the restaurant owners. Across the hall is what was once used as Mr. Wooster and his wife's bedroom. It was Ruth's bedroom in later years, and it is said that she and brother Horace lived in their respective rooms for fifteen years as the last living Woosters without speaking to each other. Why this is so is lost to history. His room was used by the Sciaraffas as a guest bedroom.

There is a large room in the rear that contains a bar at one end and is the living room space of the owners. Becoming known to many as a blatantly haunted building, the Cosmic Society of Paranormal Investigation has held seminars, monthly meetings, television appearances and formal investigations, as well as impromptu photo shoots, at the location.

Next to Horace's room is the upper end of the servants' staircase, and straight through the doorway is the back end of the service bar and a small room that once served as the servants' quarters.

The third floor of the building was used by the Woosters as two bedrooms, a playroom and a luggage compartment, and has been remodeled by the Sciaraffa family into a bedroom, a small gift shop and storage area.

It is thought that the ghosts of the Woosters are lingering due to their love of and affinity to the place. Paul himself feels a special kinship with Ruth and believes that she "acts out" or causes weird occurrences in accordance with some of his emotional states and when there are goings-on within the business or social lives that may cause stress.

Strange happenings began before the Sciaraffas opened the building as a restaurant. It seemed apparent that Ruth wanted her identity known. Her name has been written in table dust (when no one else is around or responsible) and spelled out in the attic with letters used for party decorations.

Debbie Sciaraffa remembers a time when she was in the kitchen with its door closed. The back door was closed, and the front door was locked. She heard someone knock on the front door. She opened it to find a woman and a little girl. The woman told her that her daughter could see the ghost of a woman with long gray hair sitting in a rocking chair and looking out the window of the turreted room on the third floor. The youngster said the woman's name was Ruth.

This was odd to Debbie as they hadn't opened the restaurant yet, and no one had any idea who "Ruth" was at that time. Debbie inquired, "How do you know she's a ghost?" to which the woman replied, "Because I can't see her, but my daughter can."

Debbie offered to let them have a look for themselves and, upon entering the room, said to the girl, "Do you see any ghosts, now?" to which the girl answered only, "I know they're here." They never offered their names but did say that they lived just down the street and thought they would walk over. Debbie told them they could come back anytime after the place was opened to have another look around. The owner closed the door and, without even taking her hand from the doorknob, thought that she might catch them with an afterthought as they left. She reopened the door, and the odd couple had vanished—never to be seen or heard from again. Debbie felt that there was absolutely no way they could have walked across the parking lot in such a short time.

When the restaurant first opened in November 1993, George, the cook, was surprised to feel heat generating from the ovens that he hadn't yet turned on. After preparation of a quantity of prime rib, George fed it into the oven to roast. At some time later, he checked on it, believing it should be just about done, only to discover the oven stone cold, in the off position and with the pilot light blown out.

Later that same day, George happened upon a gruesome discovery: a puddle of blood in the kitchen that trailed out to the hallway near the bar, whereupon it abruptly ended. There were four employees in the locale at that time and none had been cut or hurt. The blood was cleaned up and an explanation was never found.

Another chef, Louis, told of looking at his reflection in the window of the kitchen's swinging doors when, all of a sudden, the door swung wide open—with no one on the other side.

Paul, Debbie and one customer all heard a distinct whistle coming from the hallway outside of the bar when they were the only ones in the restaurant one evening (it happened to be November 2—All Soul's Day).

Theresa, a waitress, was once in the kitchen asking Joseph, the chef, a question. He snapped at her in an unnecessarily hostile voice. Before anyone could say anything and without any movement in the location, all of the large stirring spoons and ladles that had been hanging directly over his head fell on him. Theresa said a prayer of thanks to Ruth and quickly exited the area.

Another time, a group of friends were joking with the waiter, saying to "leave the place setting so that Ruth could join them" for their meal, and while doing so, a shrimp whizzed off of the server's tray that she had been balancing and hit one of the diners in the cheek!

There were reports of similar incidents involving requesting Ruth's presence at the dinner table for some customers. In one such case, a party of seven arrived at a reserved table, set for eight, near the front door. As waitress Anne was leading them to the table, a full glass of water flew across the table, hit the wall and smashed into pieces. They decided to allow Ruth's setting to remain on the table.

Mary, a waitress, recalls the time she had an empty soda glass placed on the center of her tray that she was holding, with her hand in the center directly under the tray. She says that she felt as if someone came up behind her and deliberately tipped the tray causing the glass to fall off and the tray to fall out of her hand.

Elizabeth, an employee, arrived for the setup of the restaurant one morning, and she and the cook were the only people in the building. He was in the kitchen doing his daily food preparations while she began to do her own. She proceeded behind the bar to retrieve an ice bucket. After bending down to get it and straightening back up, she turned around to discover herself "trapped" behind the bar as a built-in drawer had been pulled out, blocking her way. "Hey, Ruth, cut it out!" she shouted.

It was October 3, 1995, about 12:30 p.m., when two members of the kitchen crew, Sean and Jason, were working in the "hot line." Both watched as a one-gallon bucket flew toward them off the ice machine. After reporting the incident to Debbie, they returned to the kitchen to find a clean dish towel smoldering on a counter that hadn't been there before and was nowhere near the stove or any type of flame. Still, within minutes of these two events, Sean felt a tug at the base of his shirt and turned around to find nobody near him. There was another occasion in which a large full jar of mayonnaise whizzed straight toward the wall from the ice machine, nearly missing one of the cooks.

Harold, a dishwasher, was witness to a strange event while working in the upstairs bar. He heard the distinct sound of a cat's meow, and looking around immediately, he saw what he described as two glowing white eyes staring at him. Obviously frightened, he relayed the story to his co-workers, who all participated in a search for the creature that had shaken Harold up and found no trace of an animal anywhere in the structure.

David was once giving a group of three guests a tour of the house, explaining what the former uses of the rooms were when it was the Wooster estate. As the foursome reached the third floor, strains of piano music could be heard. "There is no piano in this house; where is that music coming from?" he asked the stymied trio. As they opened a door on the third floor, the music got louder, as if someone were playing the instrument right in front of them. There were no radio speakers or a piano on the third floor, but it was known that Ruth played the piano in years gone by.

On that same evening, a few patrons were about to leave the restaurant when they found that they couldn't get the front door open. David came to assist, and despite his efforts, the door would not budge. Upon checking another door as a way of exit for the customers, he found that all of the doors were inoperable. Ten minutes later, the front door opened without incident, and the confused customers left. David checked the other doors and found them to be in working order again.

Many of the varied paranormal and psychic events have occurred on Friday the thirteenth over the years. Here are two examples.

Friday, July 13, 2001: The bartender and a few patrons watched as an overturned wineglass next to the cash register slid by itself to the edge and dropped on the floor, not breaking.

It was raining outside on Friday, June 13, 1997, about 1:00 p.m., when the interior of the restaurant became overly dark. There were a total of four people in the restaurant: Paul, the owner; his lunch guest, Joyce; Edward, a chef; and the hostess, Maria.

Just after lunch, Paul left Maria, seated in the bar area, to attend to some kitchen detail, and Maria noticed a woman in a "long white dress with a high collar" walk by the kitchen doors toward the bar and turn into the Garden Room located just past the main staircase. Curious and a bit shocked, Joyce went to see who this woman was and where she went, but as she entered the same room into which she has been seen walking, there was no one there.

About one hour later, Paul decided to return a phone call to a man who had been trying to reach him. At that time, Maria received a phone call from Paul's wife, Debbie, explaining that the same man had tried phoning the restaurant but was unable to get through. Paul was having similar luck and was unable to get an outside line. Maria went to deliver Debbie's message to Paul and noticed his puzzled expression; although he was unable to make contact with an outside line, he had heard a woman's voice through the phone say "S-C-I-A-R-A-F-F-A."

Still later that same day, the normally soft background music was found blaring through the mansion's speaker system. This was "impossible" due to a master on and off volume switch, which did not allow for random variations. It took quite some time before Paul was able to adjust the volume, regardless of the switch's position.

One time, Meredith, a waitress, was tending bar and heard a glass fall at the opposite end and hit the floor. She went to clean it up and no glass could be found anywhere by herself, her co-workers and restaurant patrons, all of whom heard it fall.

Another time, Meredith was preparing for a Christmas party in Ruth's room. There was an easy listening station tuned in on the radio. All at once Meredith noticed the wings on an angel atop the mantle stop moving, and the radio changed its tune midsong to one by Guns N' Roses. The music was blaring and everyone in the restaurant could hear it.

Friends of Meredith were on the third floor with her, and as they made their way back down toward the bar area, one woman stated that they were looking for Ruth. No sooner did she utter the words when the phone receiver behind the bar flew off the hook, across the aisle and landed on the beer cooler. Within ten minutes, the softly playing music got louder and softer and then louder again. None of the controls had been tampered with.

One year on Easter, Henry parked his car in the employee lot and went to work without incident. About 9:00 p.m., Henry was walking to his car as the place had closed up earlier than usual that night. As he walked toward his car, he passed the Garden Room and noticed a group of people seated in the dark with glasses, utensils and dishes, as if in wait of being served. He was curious but knew that the restaurant was closed and decided to just go home rather than investigate further.

The next morning, he asked his co-workers what they were doing sitting in the dark. Their reply was that he was the last to leave as they had all departed about 8:30 p.m.

There are reports of all kinds of flying food and objects, sounds of breakage with nothing damaged and, at other times, objects are smashed to bits. One night a crowd at the bar watched a glass that had levitated off a table and exploded in midair. It never touched anyone or anything. When the shattered glass hit the floor, it landed in a perfect circle.

In 1997, Cosmic Society members, with psychic Joyce St. Germaine, conducted a formal investigation of the restaurant. Joyce made communication with Ruth, who related that she stays to help other spirits that are unable to cross over and for a genuine love for the place and its owners. She stays also to protect other entities that have been drawn to the dwelling—more mischievous and less content spirits.

And then there are the dimes. Hundreds and hundreds of dimes have shown up in the strangest of places over the years in the restaurant. Paul has started saving and labeling them all with dates and times, but no definitive patterns emerge; they are from all different mints, years and types. One woman was hit by a dime on her shoulder in the ladies room while washing her hands alone in there.

On one of the many tour groups I've brought to the building with Haunted Connecticut Tours, we had one woman look down at her shoe to see a dime sitting right on top of it. While talking about the subject to the group, I have had dimes whizzed or thrown directly at me in full view of everyone present. On every tour, we always ask the bus drivers to eat with us and join us on our activities if they care to or able to. On one trip, we all were inside, and during dinner I relayed tales of the haunted establishment and spoke of the dimes, even passing around the jars of them that had been collected over time. We headed back to the bus, which had been locked to safeguard people's belongings, and upon taking our seats, three people found dimes in their respective spots. This was interesting because those three had been the skeptics in our group and the ones who made light of the whole idea of ghosts (there's always at least one in every crowd and I'm used to it!). We all knew that the bus driver was the only one with key access to the vehicle and that he had been with us the entire duration. Needless to say, they didn't say much for the rest of our tour—nothing negative anyway.

On June 6, 2000, Cosmic Society invited Cablevision's show *Videoized* to be present and film our meeting held in the Carousel Gardens. It was a dark and stormy night, and the camera crew thought that was just great.

Members and guests were allowed to walk through the entire building taking photos and others of us went about setting up video cameras, electromagnetic field meters (EMF) and other detection equipment.

Just as I was about to call the meeting to order, the entire sky went dark and thunder shocks shook the building. So loud were these booms that the windows actually bowed in and out. Within seconds, we all heard a succession of earsplitting cracks. The room I was standing in was hit by lightning, and a three-foot hole was ripped into the ceiling above us. One girl, who had just joined the group as member, grabbed her keys, ran out into the storm and was never seen again by any of us.

On the second floor, the limb from the tree that was also struck smashed through the window of Ruth's room, breaking both the storm and inner window panes.

In February 2006, I was asked to film with TAPS of Syfy fame for their number one–rated TV show *Ghost Hunters* at Carousel Gardens. I had known Jason and Grant long before they became famous due to their outreach early on in each of our respective groups' beginnings. Every once in a while I'd get a call from Jason asking if "anything is up in Connecticut?" to which most times I'd reply, "Nothing worth traveling south for, you?" And he'd usually say the same. Things were slow then.

After the filming, in which absolutely nothing phenomenal happened at all, I was asked to have a picture taken with a man I didn't know and who just happened to be a patron at the bar the night of the shoot. Knowing that I didn't recognize the guy, owner Paul said, "Sure, come take a picture, I was just about to walk her out anyway." We thought it would be fitting to stand in front of the TAPS vehicle, and pictures were taken with the guy's camera

This photo shows Joe, Donna and Paul standing outside the TAPS van during filming with Syfy's hit show *Ghost Hunters*. A camera flash reflection is obvious but doesn't explain the small orb that appeared on Joe's camera film.

and then mine. What started as an orb in seconds became a misty fog in the film, and when turned sideways it seems to resemble a portrait of Henry Harrison Wooster!

Holding the Cosmic Society meetings at Carousel Gardens Restaurant over the past thirteen or so years has definitely been our pleasure. It is unfortunate that these sorry economic times have forced the building to close its doors to the public.

One other interesting thing happened just days before this printing. Winding down our monthly Cosmic Society Meeting on September 2, 2009, we were all looking at a mirror that hangs above the fireplace across from the bar. Paul had written the name "Ruth" on it in the dust with his finger last month, and folks were questioning this "paranormal event." Bursting their bubble, I quickly explained and complained that pranks like that lessen the credibility of the real in unnatural occurrences. But it was my turn to be surprised when Paul pointed out that "only the left portion of the glass, where the name was written, was literally fogged up" and very cold to the touch, whereas the right side appeared normal in every way.

Concerning photographic results, Cosmic Society has had numerous successes with spirit photography at this location with all kinds of film and cameras, as have the owners, their guests, many other investigators, amateurs and patrons of the restaurant. We've captured mists and orbs and been witness to numerable outright sightings and paranormal events. It's a veritable hotbed of otherworldly activity and in that sense truly does live up to its reputation as Connecticut's most haunted Victorian mansion, and it will always be my number one "haunted home away from home."

BIBLIOGRAPHY

Bright Lights Film Journal. "Margaret Sullavan and the Art of Dying." http://www.brightlightsfilm.com/49/sullavan.htm.

Burton, Bessie. *Friends of Boothe Park*. Brochure. Stratford, CT: Friends of Boothe Park, n.d.

Cothren, William. *History of Ancient Woodbury, Connecticut, from the first Indian deed in 1659 to 1854...including the present towns of Washington, Southbury, Bethlem, Roxbury, and a part of Oxford and Middlebury*. Waterbury, CN: Bronson Brothers, 1854–79.

Delamater, Jerome. "Sullavan, Margaret." *International Dictionary of Films and Filmmakers*. Gale Group Inc., 2001. Encyclopedia.com. http://www.encyclopedia.com/doc/1G2-3406802058.html.

Gale Research. *Encyclopedia of World Biography*, vol. 17, second edition. Farmington Mills, MI: Gale Research, 1998.

Margaret Sullavan. Answers.com. www.answers.com/topic/margaret-sullavan.

Margaret Sullavan. Who's Dated Who? www.whosdatedwho.com/celebrities/people/dating/margaret-sullavan.htm.

"Margaret Sullavan." Wikipedia, the free encyclopedia. http://en.wikipedia. org/wiki/Margaret_Sullavan.

The Society of Colonial Wars in the State of Connecticut. http://www. colonialwarsct.org/redding.htm.

Thibault, Andy. "Cool Justice: Old Murder Haunts Retired Cop." Law Tribune Newspapers. http://www.andythibault.com/columns/ cooljustice-%2003-13-06.htm.

Town of Woodbury Connecticut. Historic Glebe House. http://www. woodburyct.org/woodburyglebehouse.shtml.

Parts of the Carousel Gardens material adapted by Donna Kent from Paul and Debbie Sciaraffa, *The Adventures of Carousel Gardens* and the Carousel Gardens website: www.carouselgardens.com.

Some information was obtained from Curtis House, Connecticut's Oldest Inn, the Hardisty family and Publicans, used by permission of T.J. Brennan.

ABOUT THE AUTHOR

Donna Kent is the founder of the Cosmic Society of Paranormal Investigation and www.cosmicsociety.com, the internet's largest, free, spirit energy photo website. She has appeared on countless TV shows including Syfy's *Sightings* and *Ghost Hunters*, the *Maury Povich Show* and the ABC Special "World's Scariest Ghosts—Caught on Tape." Kent has been featured in the 2007 *New York Times* Metro Section, *Yankee* magazine, *Hartford* magazine, *New Haven* magazine and more. She has authored and published the *Investigating a Haunted Location Handbook* and has written for magazines including *Llewellyn's New World*, *Fate*, *Conscious Living* and *The Door Opener*. She is the editor and publisher of the Cosmic Connections Newsletter and the 1997, 1998 and Millennium *Ghost Calendars*. She is also featured in the 2007 *Cambridge Who's Who of Executives and Professionals*. Donna is the director of Haunted Connecticut Tours in the United States, voted Connecticut's number one tour (www.conneCTionsgrouptours.com, 866-656-0207). Cosmic Society offers worldwide membership, classes, workshops, seminars and presentations on spirit photography and paranormal investigation. Donna can be reached at 203-463-8300 or at donnakentcosmicsociety@gmail.com. Please visit her on the web at www.CosmicSociety.com.

Visit us at
www.historypress.net